kubectl: Command-Line Kubernetes in a Nutshell

Deploy, manage, and debug container workloads using the Kubernetes CLI

Rimantas Mocevicius

BIRMINGHAM—MUMBAI

kubectl: Command-Line Kubernetes in a Nutshell

Commissioning Editor: Mohd Riyan Khan

Acquisition Editor: Savia Lobo

Senior Editor: Arun Nadar

Content Development Editor: Romy Dias

Technical Editor: Soham Amburle

Copy Editor: Safis Editing

Project Coordinator: Neil Dmello

Proofreader: Safis Editing

Indexer: Rekha Nair

Production Designer: Vijay Kamble

First published: October 2020

Production reference: 1221020

Published by Packt Publishing Ltd.
Livery Place
35 Livery Street
Birmingham
B3 2PB, UK.

ISBN 978-1-80056-187-8

www.packt.com

Packt.com

Subscribe to our online digital library for full access to over 7,000 books and videos, as well as industry leading tools to help you plan your personal development and advance your career. For more information, please visit our website.

Why subscribe?

- Spend less time learning and more time coding with practical eBooks and Videos from over 4,000 industry professionals

- Improve your learning with Skill Plans built especially for you

- Get a free eBook or video every month

- Fully searchable for easy access to vital information

- Copy and paste, print, and bookmark content

Did you know that Packt offers eBook versions of every book published, with PDF and ePub files available? You can upgrade to the eBook version at packt.com and as a print book customer, you are entitled to a discount on the eBook copy. Get in touch with us at customercare@packtpub.com for more details.

At www.packt.com, you can also read a collection of free technical articles, sign up for a range of free newsletters, and receive exclusive discounts and offers on Packt books and eBooks.

Contributors

About the author

Rimantas Mocevicius is an IT professional with over 25 years' experience in DevOps, which includes Linux, containers, Kubernetes, and cloud-native technologies. He is also co-founded Helm – the Kubernetes package manager.

Since 2018 he has worked at JFrog Ltd (Nasdaq: FROG) as a senior software engineer in the Community Engineering team, which supports community-related centers such as GoCenter, ConanCenter, and ChartCenter. The centers help the open source community to adopt Go packages, C/C++ packages, and Helm charts.

He is a big fan and supporter of open source software. His passion for new technologies drives him forward, and he never wants to stop learning about them.

Twitter: `Rimusz`

LinkedIn: Rimantas Mocevicius

I would like to say very huge thank you my wife Vilma for all her support while I was writing the book, and for giving me the space and time to complete it on time.

Also, I would like to say a big thank you to the technical reviewer, Eldad Assis, for his invaluable recommendations. He is also an amazing colleague of mine at JFrog.

Lots of thanks to the Packt Publishing editing team for all the help they provided while I was writing the book, and especially to Romy Dias for pushing me to the last mile to make it better.

About the reviewer

Eldad Assis is an experienced developer who turned into an infrastructure geek about 20 years ago. Linux, automation, CI/CD, cloud-native, and DevOps principles have been key parts of his professional life. He takes applications to the public cloud, from simple virtual machines all the way to containerized microservices in Kubernetes.

He advocates DevOps practices and implements cloud-native principles for a living.

Today, he's a DevOps architect at JFrog, mostly working on leading the journey to cloud-native microservices in Kubernetes in public clouds as part of JFrog's SaaS offering.

Twitter: `eldadak`

LinkedIn: Eldad Assis

Packt is searching for authors like you

If you're interested in becoming an author for Packt, please visit `authors.packtpub.com` and apply today. We have worked with thousands of developers and tech professionals, just like you, to help them share their insight with the global tech community. You can make a general application, apply for a specific hot topic that we are recruiting an author for, or submit your own idea.

Table of Contents

3

Working with Nodes

Section 3: Application Management

4

Creating and Deploying Applications

5

Updating and Deleting Applications

6

Debugging an Application

Section 4:
Extending kubectl

7
Working with kubectl Plugins

8
Introducing Kustomize for Kubernetes

9
Introducing Helm for Kubernetes

10
kubectl Best Practices and Docker Commands

Other Books You May Enjoy

Index

Preface

This book is a comprehensive introduction for those who are new to Kubernetes management via the command line that will get you up to speed in no time.

Kubernetes is an open source container orchestration system for automating application deployment, scaling, and management, and `kubectl` is a command-line tool that helps to manage it.

Who this book is for

This book is for DevOps, developers, system administrators, and all the people in between who wish to use the `kubectl` command line to perform Kubernetes functionalities, who maybe know Docker but haven't mastered using `kubectl` to deploy containers to Kubernetes.

What this book covers

Chapter 1, *Introducing and Installing kubectl*, provides a brief overview of `kubectl` and how to install and set it up.

Chapter 2, *Getting Information about a Cluster*, teaches the reader how to get info about a cluster and the available API list.

Chapter 3, *Working with Nodes*, teaches the reader how to get info about the cluster nodes.

Chapter 4, *Creating and Deploying Applications*, explains how to create and install Kubernetes applications.

Chapter 5, *Updating and Deleting Applications*, explains how to update Kubernetes applications.

Chapter 6, *Debugging an Application*, explains how to view application logs, `exec` to container

Chapter 7, *Working with kubectl Plugins*, explains how to install `kubectl` plugins.

Chapter 8, Introducing Kustomize for kubectl, discusses Kustomize.

Chapter 9, Introducing Helm for Kubernetes, discusses Helm, the Kubernetes package manager.

Chapter 10, kubectl Best Practices and Docker Commands, covers `kubectl` best practices and Docker equivalents in `kubectl`.

To get the most out of this book

Software/Hardware covered in the book	OS Requirements
Kubernetes cluster	Windows, macOS X, and Linux (any of these)
kubectl	Windows, macOS X, and Linux (any of these)
Helm	Windows, macOS X, and Linux (any of these)

We recommend accessing the code via the GitHub repository (link available in the next section). Doing so will help you avoid any potential errors related to the copying and pasting of code.

Download the example code files

You can download the example code files for this book from GitHub at `https://github.com/PacktPublishing/kubectl-Command-Line-Kubernetes-in-a-Nutshell`. In case there's an update to the code, it will be updated on the existing GitHub repository.

We also have other code bundles from our rich catalog of books and videos available at `https://github.com/PacktPublishing/`. Check them out!

Download the color images

We also provide a PDF file that has color images of the screenshots/diagrams used in this book. You can download it here: `https://static.packt-cdn.com/downloads/9781800561878_ColorImages.pdf`.

Conventions used

There are a number of text conventions used throughout this book.

`Code in text`: Indicates code words in text, database table names, folder names, filenames, file extensions, pathnames, dummy URLs, user input, and Twitter handles. Here is an example: "Create the `.kube` directory in your home directory."

A block of code is set as follows:

```
apiVersion: apps/v1
kind: Deployment
metadata:
  name: postgresql
  labels:
    app: postgresql
```

When we wish to draw your attention to a particular part of a code block, the relevant lines or items are set in bold:

```
spec:
  replicas: 1
  selector:
    matchLabels:
      app: postgresql
```

Any command-line input or output is written as follows:

```
$ kubectl version –client --short
Client Version: v1.18.1
```

Bold: Indicates a new term, an important word, or words that you see onscreen. For example, words in menus or dialog boxes appear in the text like this. Here is an example: "We assigned **Labels** and **Annotations** to the node, and there are no **Roles** or **Taints** set."

> **Tips or important notes**
> Appear like this.

Get in touch

Feedback from our readers is always welcome.

General feedback: If you have questions about any aspect of this book, mention the book title in the subject of your message and email us at customercare@packtpub.com.

Errata: Although we have taken every care to ensure the accuracy of our content, mistakes do happen. If you have found a mistake in this book, we would be grateful if you would report this to us. Please visit www.packtpub.com/support/errata, selecting your book, clicking on the Errata Submission Form link, and entering the details.

Piracy: If you come across any illegal copies of our works in any form on the Internet, we would be grateful if you would provide us with the location address or website name. Please contact us at copyright@packt.com with a link to the material.

If you are interested in becoming an author: If there is a topic that you have expertise in and you are interested in either writing or contributing to a book, please visit authors.packtpub.com.

Reviews

Please leave a review. Once you have read and used this book, why not leave a review on the site that you purchased it from? Potential readers can then see and use your unbiased opinion to make purchase decisions, we at Packt can understand what you think about our products, and our authors can see your feedback on their book. Thank you!

For more information about Packt, please visit packt.com.

Section 1: Getting Started with kubectl

In this section, you will learn what kubectl is and how to install it.

This section contains the following chapter:

- *Chapter 1, Introducing and Installing kubectl*

1
Introducing and Installing kubectl

Kubernetes is an open source container orchestration system for managing containerized applications across multiple hosts in a cluster.

Kubernetes provides mechanisms for application deployment, scheduling, updating, maintenance, and scaling. A key feature of Kubernetes is that it actively manages containers to ensure that the state of the cluster always matches the user's expectations.

Kubernetes enables you to respond quickly to customer demand by scaling or rolling out new features. It also allows you to make full use of your hardware.

Kubernetes is the following:

- **Lean**: Lightweight, simple, and accessible
- **Portable**: Public, private, hybrid, and multi-cloud
- **Extensible**: Modular, pluggable, hookable, composable, and toolable
- **Self-healing**: Auto-placement, auto-restart, and auto-replication

Kubernetes builds on a decade and a half of experience at Google running production workloads at scale, combined with best-of-breed ideas and best practices from the community:

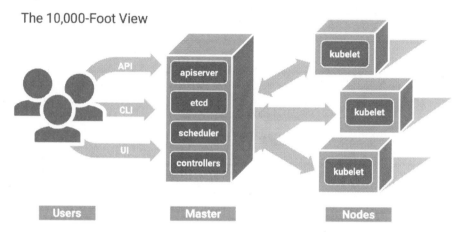

Figure 1.1 – A 10,000-foot view of Kubernetes' architecture

One of the ways to manage Kubernetes clusters is kubectl—Kubernetes' command-line tool for management, it is a tool for accessing a Kubernetes cluster that allows you to run different commands against Kubernetes clusters to deploy apps, manage nodes, troubleshoot deployments, and more.

In this chapter, we're going to cover the following main topics:

- Introducing kubectl
- Installing kubectl
- kubectl commands

Technical requirements

To learn kubectl, you will need access to a Kubernetes cluster; it can be one of these cloud ones:

- Google Cloud GKE: https://cloud.google.com/kubernetes-engine
- Azure AKS EKS: https://azure.microsoft.com/en-us/free/kubernetes-service
- AWS EKS: https://aws.amazon.com/eks/
- DigitalOcean DOKS: https://www.digitalocean.com/docs/kubernetes/

Alternatively, it can be a local one:

- KIND: `https://kind.sigs.k8s.io/docs/user/quick-start/`
- Minikube: `https://kubernetes.io/docs/setup/learning-environment/minikube/`
- Docker Desktop: `https://www.docker.com/products/docker-desktop`

In this book, we are going to use Google Cloud's GKE Kubernetes cluster.

Introducing kubectl

You can use `kubectl` to deploy applications, inspect and manage them, check cluster resources, view logs, and more.

`kubectl` is a command-line tool that can run from your computer, in CI/CD pipelines, as part of the operating system, or as a Docker image. It is a very automation-friendly tool.

`kubectl` looks for a configuration file named `.kube` in the `$HOME` folder. In the `.kube` file, `kubectl` stores the cluster configurations needed to access a Kubernetes cluster. You can also set the `KUBECONFIG` environment variable or use the `--kubeconfig` flag to point to the `kubeconfig` file.

Installing kubectl

Let's take a look at how you can install `kubectl` on macOS, on Windows, and in CI/CD pipelines.

Installing on macOS

The easiest way to install `kubectl` on macOS is using the Homebrew package manager (`https://brew.sh/`):

1. To install, run this:

   ```
   $ brew install kubectl
   ```

2. To see the version you have installed, use this:

   ```
   $ kubectl version -client --short
   Client Version: v1.18.1
   ```

Installing on Windows

To install `kubectl` on Windows, you could use the simple command-line installer Scoop (`https://scoop.sh/`):

1. To install, run this:

    ```
    $ scoop install kubectl
    ```

2. To see the version you have installed, use this:

    ```
    $ kubectl version -client --short
    Client Version: v1.18.1
    ```

3. Create the `.kube` directory in your home directory:

    ```
    $ mkdir %USERPROFILE%\.kube
    ```

4. Navigate to the `.kube` directory:

    ```
    $ cd %USERPROFILE%\.kube
    ```

5. Configure `kubectl` to use a remote Kubernetes cluster:

    ```
    $ New-Item config -type file
    ```

Installing on Linux

When you want to use `kubectl` on Linux, you have two options:

*   Use `curl`:

    ```
    $ curl -LO https://storage.googleapis.com/kubernetes-
    release/release/`curl -s https://storage.googleapis.com/
    kubernetes-release/release/stable.txt`/bin/linux/amd64/
    kubectl
    ```

*   If your Linux system supports Docker images, use `https://hub.docker.com/r/bitnami/kubectl/`.

    > **Note**
    >
    > Linux is a very common environment for CI/CD pipelines.

kubectl commands

To get a list of supported `kubectl` commands, run this:

```
$ kubectl --help
```

`kubectl` commands are grouped by category. Let's look at each category.

Basic commands

The following are basic `kubectl` commands:

- `create`: Create a resource from a file or from `stdin`; for example, create a Kubernetes deployment from the file.
- `expose`: Take a service, deployment, or pod and expose it as a new Kubernetes Service.
- `run`: Run a particular image on the cluster.
- `set`: Set specific features on objects—for example, set environment variables, update a Docker image in a pod template, and so on.
- `explain`: Get the documentation of resources—for example, the documentation on deployments.
- `get`: Display one or many resources. For example, you can get a list of running pods or the YAML output of a pod.
- `edit`: Edit a resource—for example, edit a deployment.
- `delete`: Delete resources by filenames, `stdin`, resources, and names, or by resources and label selectors.

Deploy commands

The following are `kubectl` deploy commands:

- `rollout`: Manage the rollout of a resource.
- `scale`: Set a new size for a deployment, ReplicaSet, or StatefulSet.
- `autoscale`: Auto-scale a deployment, ReplicaSet, or StatefulSet.

Cluster management commands

The following are the `kubectl` cluster management commands:

- `certificate`: Modify certificate resources.

- `cluster-info`: Display cluster information.

- `top`: Display resource (CPU/memory/storage) usage.

- `cordon`: Mark a node as unschedulable.

- `uncordon`: Mark a node as schedulable.

- `drain`: Drain a node in preparation for maintenance.

- `taint`: Update the taints on one or more nodes.

Troubleshooting and debugging commands

The following are the `kubectl` troubleshooting and debugging commands:

- `describe`: Show the details of a specific resource or group of resources.

- `logs`: Print the logs for a container in a pod.

- `attach`: Attach to a running container.

- `exec`: Execute a command in a container.

- `port-forward`: Forward one or more local ports to a pod.

- `proxy`: Run a proxy to the Kubernetes API server.

- `cp`: Copy files and directories to and from containers.

- `auth`: Inspect authorization.

Advanced commands

The following are the `kubectl` advanced commands:

- `diff`: Show difference of live version against a would-be applied version.

- `apply`: Apply a configuration to a resource by filename or `stdin`.

- `patch`: Update the field(s) of a resource using a strategic merge patch.

- `replace`: Replace a resource by filename or `stdin`.

- `wait`: Wait for a specific condition on one or many resources.

- `convert`: Convert config files between different API versions.
- `kustomize`: Build a kustomization target from a directory or a remote URL.

Settings commands

The following are the settings commands in `kubectl`:

- `label`: Update the labels on a resource.
- `annotate`: Update the annotations on a resource.

Other commands

The following are several other commands used in `kubectl`:

- `alpha`: Commands for features in alpha.
- `api-resources`: Print the supported API resources on the server.
- `api-versions`: Print the supported API versions on the server, in the form of group/version.
- `config`: Modify `kube-config` files.
- `plugin`: Provide utilities for interacting with plugins.
- `version`: Print the client and server version information.

As you can see from the lists, commands are divided into different groups. We are going to learn about most but not all of these commands in the coming chapters.

At the time of writing, the `kubectl` version is 1.18; with more recent versions, the commands might have changed.

Summary

In this chapter, we have learned what `kubectl` is and how to install it on macOS, Windows, and CI/CD pipelines. We also checked out the different commands supported by `kubectl` and what they do.

In the next chapter, we will learn how to get information about Kubernetes clusters using `kubectl`.

Section 2: Kubernetes Cluster and Node Management

This section explains how to manage Kubernetes clusters, how to get information about clusters and nodes, and how to work with nodes.

This section contains the following chapters:

- *Chapter 2, Getting Information about a Cluster*
- *Chapter 3, Working with Nodes*

2
Getting Information about a Cluster

When you are managing a Kubernetes cluster, it is necessary to know what Kubernetes version it is running on, the details about the master (also called the control plane), any addons installed on the cluster, and the available APIs and resources. As different Kubernetes versions support different API versions for resources, not setting the right/ unsupported API version for your, for example, Ingress, will cause the deployment to fail.

In this chapter, we're going to cover the following topics:

- Cluster information
- Cluster API versions
- Cluster API resources

Cluster information

It is always good to know which version of the Kubernetes server (API) is installed for a Kubernetes cluster as you might want to use particular features available in that version. To check the server version, run the following:

```
$ kubectl version --short
Client Version: v1.18.1
Server Version: v1.17.5-gke.9
```

The server version is `v1.17.5` and the `kubectl` version is `v1.18.1`. Note that the `-gke.9` bit of the server version is the internal GKE revision; as we mentioned earlier, for the book's purposes, a GKE cluster is used.

> **Important note**
>
> The `kubectl` version can be a more recent one; it does not really have to match the server version, as the latest version is usually backward compatible. However, it is not recommended to use an older `kubectl` version with a more recent server version.

Next, let's check the cluster server information by running the following command:

```
$ kubectl cluster-info
Kubernetes master is running at https://35.223.200.75
GLBCDefaultBackend is running at https://35.223.200.75/api/v1/
namespaces/kube-system/services/default-http-backend:http/proxy
KubeDNS is running at https://35.223.200.75/api/v1/namespaces/
kube-system/services/kube-dns:dns/proxy
Metrics-server is running at https://35.223.200.75/api/v1/
namespaces/kube-system/services/https:metrics-server:/proxy
```

In the preceding output log, we see the following:

- The master endpoint IP (`35.223.200.75`), where your `kubectl` connects to the Kubernetes API.

- A list of installed addons, which in this setup are more GKE cluster-specific:

  a. `GLBDefaultBackend`

  b. `KubeDNS`

  c. `Metrics-server`

The addons list will vary between cloud-based and on-premises installations.

Finally, let's check cluster node information using the following command:

```
$ kubectl get nodes
```

The output of the preceding command is as shown in the following screenshot:

NAME	STATUS	ROLES	AGE	VERSION
gke-kubectl-lab-we-app-pool-1302ab74-7bbf	Ready	<none>	2m7s	v1.17.8-gke.17
gke-kubectl-lab-we-app-pool-1302ab74-hlpz	Ready	<none>	2m7s	v1.17.8-gke.17
gke-kubectl-lab-we-app-pool-1302ab74-zgwx	Ready	<none>	2m8s	v1.17.8-gke.17

Figure 2.1 – Output showing node information

The preceding command shows a list of the nodes available in the cluster with their status and Kubernetes version.

Cluster API versions

It is good practice to check the available cluster API versions because each new Kubernetes version usually brings with it new API versions and deprecates/removes some old ones.

To get an API list, run the following command:

```
$ kubectl api-versions
```

The output for the preceding command gives us a list of APIs, as shown in the following screenshot:

```
admissionregistration.k8s.io/v1
admissionregistration.k8s.io/v1beta1
apiextensions.k8s.io/v1
apiextensions.k8s.io/v1beta1
apiregistration.k8s.io/v1
apiregistration.k8s.io/v1beta1
apps/v1
authentication.k8s.io/v1
authentication.k8s.io/v1beta1
authorization.k8s.io/v1
authorization.k8s.io/v1beta1
autoscaling/v1
autoscaling/v2beta1
autoscaling/v2beta2
batch/v1
batch/v1beta1
certificates.k8s.io/v1beta1
cloud.google.com/v1
cloud.google.com/v1beta1
coordination.k8s.io/v1
coordination.k8s.io/v1beta1
discovery.k8s.io/v1beta1
extensions/v1beta1
metrics.k8s.io/v1beta1
migration.k8s.io/v1alpha1
networking.gke.io/v1beta1
networking.gke.io/v1beta2
networking.k8s.io/v1
networking.k8s.io/v1beta1
node.k8s.io/v1beta1
nodemanagement.gke.io/v1alpha1
policy/v1beta1
rbac.authorization.k8s.io/v1
rbac.authorization.k8s.io/v1beta1
scalingpolicy.kope.io/v1alpha1
scheduling.k8s.io/v1
scheduling.k8s.io/v1beta1
snapshot.storage.k8s.io/v1beta1
storage.k8s.io/v1
storage.k8s.io/v1beta1
v1
```

Figure 2.2 – API list

You need to know which APIs can be used in your application, as otherwise, the deployment could fail if the API version you use is not supported anymore.

Cluster resources list

Another handy list is the resources list, which shows the available resources, their short names (to use with kubectl), the API group a resource belongs to, whether a resource is namespaced or not, and the KIND type.

To get the resources list, run the following command:

```
$ kubectl api-resources
```

The preceding command gives us the following list of resources:

```
NAME                               SHORTNAMES     APIGROUP                      NAMESPACED    KIND
bindings                                                                        true          Binding
componentstatuses                  cs                                           false         ComponentStatus
configmaps                         cm                                           true          ConfigMap
endpoints                          ep                                           true          Endpoints
events                             ev                                           true          Event
limitranges                        limits                                       true          LimitRange
namespaces                         ns                                           false         Namespace
nodes                              no                                           false         Node
persistentvolumeclaims             pvc                                          true          PersistentVolumeClaim
persistentvolumes                  pv                                           false         PersistentVolume
pods                               po                                           true          Pod
podtemplates                                                                    true          PodTemplate
replicationcontrollers             rc                                           true          ReplicationController
resourcequotas                     quota                                        true          ResourceQuota
secrets                                                                         true          Secret
serviceaccounts                    sa                                           true          ServiceAccount
services                           svc                                          true          Service
mutatingwebhookconfigurations                     admissionregistration.k8s.io  false         MutatingWebhookConfiguration
validatingwebhookconfigurations                   admissionregistration.k8s.io  false         ValidatingWebhookConfiguration
customresourcedefinitions          crd,crds       apiextensions.k8s.io          false         CustomResourceDefinition
apiservices                                        apiregistration.k8s.io        false         APIService
```

Figure 2.3 – List of resources

As the list is quite long, we are only showing part of it in the preceding screenshot.

Getting a list of resources will help you to run kubectl commands using short resource names and to know which API group a resource belongs to.

Summary

In this chapter, we have learned how to use kubectl to get information about a Kubernetes cluster, the available APIs, and the API resources in a cluster.

In the next chapter, we are going to look at how to get information about the nodes present in a Kubernetes cluster.

3

Working with Nodes

Everyone familiar with Kubernetes knows that the cluster workload runs in nodes, where all Kubernetes pods get scheduled, deployed, redeployed, and destroyed.

Kubernetes runs the workload by placing containers into pods and then schedules them to run on nodes. A node might be a virtual or physical machine, depending on the cluster setup. Each node has the services necessary to run pods, managed by the Kubernetes control plane.

The main components of the node are as follows:

- **kubelet**: An agent that registers/deregisters the node with the Kubernetes API.
- **Container runtime**: This runs containers.
- **kube-proxy**: Network proxy.

If the Kubernetes cluster supports nodes autoscaling, then nodes can come and go as specified by the autoscaling rules: by setting min and max node counts. If there is not much load running in the cluster, unnecessary nodes will be removed down to the minimum nodes set by the autoscaling rules. And when the load increases, the required amount of nodes will be deployed to accommodate the newly scheduled pods.

There are times when you need to troubleshoot, get information about the nodes in the cluster, find out which pods they are running, see how much CPU and memory they are consuming, and so on.

There are always going to be cases when you need to stop scheduling pods on some nodes, or rescheduling pods to different nodes, or temporally disabling the scheduling of any pods to some nodes, removing nodes, or any other reasons.

In this chapter, we're going to cover the following main topics:

- Getting a list of nodes
- Describing nodes
- Displaying node resource usage
- Cordoning nodes
- Draining nodes
- Removing nodes
- Introduction to node pools

Getting a list of nodes

To start working with nodes, you need to get a list of them first. To get the nodes list, run the following command:

```
$ kubectl get nodes
```

We get the following list of nodes using the preceding command:

```
NAME                                          STATUS   ROLES    AGE     VERSION
gke-kubectl-lab-default-pool-b3c7050d-6s1l    Ready    <none>   172m    v1.17.5-gke.9
gke-kubectl-lab-default-pool-b3c7050d-8jhj    Ready    <none>   6h33m   v1.17.5-gke.9
gke-kubectl-lab-default-pool-b3c7050d-d2lr    Ready    <none>   6h33m   v1.17.5-gke.9
```

Figure 3.1 – Nodes list

The preceding list shows we have three nodes in our Kubernetes cluster with a Ready status and Kubernetes version 1.17.5-gke.9. However, if you have cloud-supported node pools with autoscaling, your nodes list could be different because nodes will be added/removed depending on the number of applications running in your cluster.

Describing nodes

The `kubectl describe` command allows us to get the state, metadata, and events of an object in a Kubernetes cluster. In this section, we will use it to describe the node.

We have got a list of nodes, so let's check out one of them:

1. To describe a node, run the following command:

    ```
    $ kubectl describe node gke-kubectl-lab-default-pool-
    b3c7050d-6s1l
    ```

    As the command's output is quite big, we are going to show only some parts of it. You can check out the full output yourself.

2. In the following screenshot, we see the assigned `Labels` (which can be used to organize and select subsets of objects) and `Annotations` (extra information about the node is stored there) for the node, and `Unschedulable: false` means that the node accepts pods to be scheduled on to it. For example, `Labels` can be used for `Node Affinity` (which allows us to constrain which nodes the pod is eligible to be scheduled on, based on the labels on the node) to schedule pods on particular nodes:

```
Name:              gke-kubectl-lab-default-pool-b3c7050d-6s1l
Roles:             <none>
Labels:            beta.kubernetes.io/arch=amd64
                   beta.kubernetes.io/instance-type=n1-standard-1
                   beta.kubernetes.io/os=linux
                   cloud.google.com/gke-nodepool=default-pool
                   cloud.google.com/gke-os-distribution=cos
                   cloud.google.com/gke-preemptible=true
                   failure-domain.beta.kubernetes.io/region=us-central1
                   failure-domain.beta.kubernetes.io/zone=us-central1-c
                   kubernetes.io/arch=amd64
                   kubernetes.io/hostname=gke-kubectl-lab-default-pool-b3c7050d-6s1l
                   kubernetes.io/os=linux
                   node.kubernetes.io/instance-type=n1-standard-1
                   topology.kubernetes.io/region=us-central1
                   topology.kubernetes.io/zone=us-central1-c
Annotations:       container.googleapis.com/instance_id: 1280108996065801395
                   node.alpha.kubernetes.io/ttl: 0
                   volumes.kubernetes.io/controller-managed-attach-detach: true
CreationTimestamp: Sat, 13 Jun 2020 17:13:46 +0300
Taints:            <none>
Unschedulable:     false
```

Figure 3.2 – Node describe – check labels and annotations

3. In the following screenshot, we see the assigned internal and external IPs, the internal DNS name, and the hostname:

```
Addresses:
  InternalIP:    10.128.0.32
  ExternalIP:    34.72.251.139
  InternalDNS:   gke-kubectl-lab-default-pool-b3c7050d-6s1l.c.rimusz-lab1.internal
  Hostname:      gke-kubectl-lab-default-pool-b3c7050d-6s1l.c.rimusz-lab1.internal
Capacity:
  attachable-volumes-gce-pd:  127
  cpu:                        1
  ephemeral-storage:          98868448Ki
  hugepages-2Mi:              0
  memory:                     3785960Ki
  pods:                       55
```

Figure 3.3 – Node describe – assigned internal and external IPs

4. The following screenshot shows the running pods on the node with CPU/memory requests and limits per pod:

Non-terminated Pods:	(4 in total)					
Namespace	Name	CPU Requests	CPU Limits	Memory Requests	Memory Limits	AGE
---------	----	------------	----------	---------------	-------------	---
kube-system	fluentd-gke-cqbqp	0 (0%)	0 (0%)	0 (0%)	0 (0%)	4h24m
kube-system	gke-metrics-agent-lp7c6	2m (0%)	0 (0%)	20Mi (0%)	50Mi (1%)	4h24m
kube-system	kube-proxy-gke-kubectl-lab-default-pool-b3c7050d-6s1l	100m (10%)	0 (0%)	0 (0%)	0 (0%)	4h24m
kube-system	prometheus-to-sd-mmvjm	0 (0%)	0 (0%)	0 (0%)	0 (0%)	4h24m

Figure 3.4 – Node describe – CPU/memory requests and limits per pod

5. The following screenshot shows the allocated resources for the node:

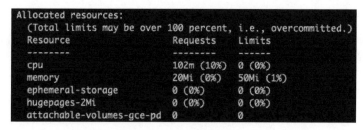

```
Allocated resources:
  (Total limits may be over 100 percent, i.e., overcommitted.)
  Resource                    Requests      Limits
  --------                    --------      ------
  cpu                         102m (10%)    0 (0%)
  memory                      20Mi (0%)     50Mi (1%)
  ephemeral-storage           0 (0%)        0 (0%)
  hugepages-2Mi               0 (0%)        0 (0%)
  attachable-volumes-gce-pd   0             0
```

Figure 3.5 – Node describe – allocated resources for the node

As you can see, the $ kubectl describe node command allows you to get various information about the node.

Displaying node resource usage

It is handy to know what resources are consumed by nodes. To display the resources used by nodes, run the following command:

```
$ kubectl top nodes
```

We get the following list of nodes using the preceding command:

```
NAME                                       CPU(cores)   CPU%   MEMORY(bytes)   MEMORY%
gke-kubectl-lab-default-pool-b3c7050d-6s1l   45m         4%     570Mi           21%
gke-kubectl-lab-default-pool-b3c7050d-8jhj   49m         5%     703Mi           26%
gke-kubectl-lab-default-pool-b3c7050d-d2lr   50m         5%     680Mi           25%
```

Figure 3.6 – Top nodes list with resources used

The previous command shows node metrics such as CPU cores, memory (in bytes), and CPU and memory percentage usage.

Also, by using $ watch kubectl top nodes, you can watch and monitor nodes in real time when, for example, load testing your application or doing other node operations.

> **Note**
>
> The watch command might not be present in your computer, you might need to install it. The watch command will run the specified command and refresh the screen every few seconds.

Cordoning nodes

Let's suppose we are going to run an app's load test and we want to keep a node away from the load test. In the node list that we saw in the *Getting a list of nodes* section, we have three nodes, and they are all in the Ready state. Let's pick one node, gke-kubectl-lab-default-pool-b3c7050d-8jhj, which we do not want new pods to be scheduled on.

kubectl has a command called cordon, which allows us to make a node unschedulable:

```
$ kubectl cordon -h
Mark node as unschedulable.
Examples:
  # Mark node "foo" as unschedulable.
  kubectl cordon foo
Options:
      --dry-run='none': Must be "none", "server", or "client".
```

```
If client strategy, only print the object that would be
sent, without sending it. If server strategy, submit server-
side request without persisting the resource.
    -l, --selector='': Selector (label query) to filter on
Usage:
    kubectl cordon NODE [options]
```

Let's cordon the gke-kubectl-lab-default-pool-b3c7050d-8jhj node and then print a nodes list. To cordon the node, run the following:

```
$ kubectl cordon gke-kubectl-lab-default-pool-b3c7050d-8jhj
```

We get the following output after running the preceding command:

```
~ $ kubectl cordon gke-kubectl-lab-default-pool-b3c7050d-8jhj
node/gke-kubectl-lab-default-pool-b3c7050d-8jhj already cordoned
~ $ kubectl get nodes
NAME                                          STATUS                   ROLES    AGE   VERSION
gke-kubectl-lab-default-pool-b3c7050d-6s1l    Ready                    <none>   17h   v1.17.5-gke.9
gke-kubectl-lab-default-pool-b3c7050d-8jhj    Ready,SchedulingDisabled <none>   28h   v1.17.5-gke.9
gke-kubectl-lab-default-pool-b3c7050d-d2lr    Ready                    <none>   13h   v1.17.5-gke.9
```

Figure 3.8 – Cordoning nodes

We have cordoned the gke-kubectl-lab-default-pool-b3c7050d-8jhj node so from now on, no new pods will be scheduled onto that node, but whatever pods are running there will stay running on that node.

> **Important note**
> If the cordoned node gets rebooted then all pods that were scheduled on it will get rescheduled to different nodes, as even when rebooting the node its readiness status doesn't change.

If we want the node to be scheduled on again, you just use uncordon command. To uncordon the node, run the following command:

```
$ kubectl uncordon gke-kubectl-lab-default-pool-b3c7050d-8jhj
```

We get the following output after running the preceding command:

```
~ $ kubectl uncordon gke-kubectl-lab-default-pool-b3c7050d-8jhj
node/gke-kubectl-lab-default-pool-b3c7050d-8jhj already uncordoned
~ $ kubectl get nodes
NAME                                          STATUS   ROLES    AGE    VERSION
gke-kubectl-lab-default-pool-b3c7050d-6s1l    Ready    <none>   115m   v1.17.5-gke.9
gke-kubectl-lab-default-pool-b3c7050d-8jhj    Ready    <none>   9h     v1.17.5-gke.9
gke-kubectl-lab-default-pool-b3c7050d-d2lr    Ready    <none>   37m    v1.17.5-gke.9
```

Figure 3.9 – Uncordoning nodes

As you can see from the preceding screenshot, the `gke-kubectl-lab-default-pool-b3c7050d-8jhj` node is in the `Ready` state again and new pods will be scheduled on it from now on.

Draining nodes

You might want to remove/evict all pods from a node that is going to be deleted, upgraded, or rebooted, for example. There is a command, `drain`, for that. Its output is quite long, so only some of the output will be shown:

```
$ kubectl drain -help
```

We get the following output from the preceding command:

```
Drain node in preparation for maintenance.

 The given node will be marked unschedulable to prevent new pods from arriving. 'drain' evicts the pods if the APIServer
supportshttp://kubernetes.io/docs/admin/disruptions/ . Otherwise, it will use normal DELETE to delete the pods. The
'drain' evicts or deletes all pods except mirror pods (which cannot be deleted through the API server).  If there are
DaemonSet-managed pods, drain will not proceed without --ignore-daemonsets, and regardless it will not delete any
DaemonSet-managed pods, because those pods would be immediately replaced by the DaemonSet controller, which ignores
unschedulable markings.  If there are any pods that are neither mirror pods nor managed by ReplicationController,
ReplicaSet, DaemonSet, StatefulSet or Job, then drain will not delete any pods unless you use --force.  --force will
also allow deletion to proceed if the managing resource of one or more pods is missing.
```

Figure 3.10 – Partial kubectl drain – help output

As you can see from the output, there are a few flags you need to pass to properly drain the node: `--ignore-daemonsets` and `-force`.

> **Note**
> A DaemonSet ensures that all specified Kubernetes nodes run a copy of the same pod specified in the DaemonSet. A DaemonSet cannot be deleted from the Kubernetes node, so the `--ignore-daemonsets` flag must be used to force draining the node.

Let's drain the `gke-kubectl-lab-default-pool-b3c7050d-8jhj` node using the following command:

```
$ kubectl drain gke-kubectl-lab-default-pool-b3c7050d-8jhj
--ignore-daemonsets -force
```

We drain the node using the preceding command. The output of this command is as shown in the following screenshot:

```
~ $ kubectl drain gke-kubectl-lab-default-pool-b3c7050d-8jhj --ignore-daemonsets --force
node/gke-kubectl-lab-default-pool-b3c7050d-8jhj cordoned
WARNING: ignoring DaemonSet-managed Pods: kube-system/fluentd-gke-w57s5, kube-system/gke-metrics-agent-bd9bd
evicting pod kube-system/event-exporter-gke-6c56555957-4b72r
evicting pod kube-system/stackdriver-metadata-agent-cluster-level-7c964f8557-hbh9j
evicting pod kube-system/kube-dns-5c9ff9fc54-gbs99
pod/stackdriver-metadata-agent-cluster-level-7c964f8557-hbh9j evicted
pod/kube-dns-5c9ff9fc54-gbs99 evicted
pod/event-exporter-gke-6c56555957-4b72r evicted
node/gke-kubectl-lab-default-pool-b3c7050d-8jhj evicted
~ $ kubectl get nodes
NAME                                          STATUS                   ROLES    AGE    VERSION
gke-kubectl-lab-default-pool-b3c7050d-6s1l    Ready                    <none>   171m   v1.17.5-gke.9
gke-kubectl-lab-default-pool-b3c7050d-8jhj    Ready,SchedulingDisabled <none>   10h    v1.17.5-gke.9
gke-kubectl-lab-default-pool-b3c7050d-d2lr    Ready                    <none>   94m    v1.17.5-gke.9
```

Figure 3.11 – Drain node

> **Important note**
>
> We have passed the --ignore-daemonsets flag so that if there are any DaemonSets running on the node the drain command will not fail.

So, we have drained the node. What else does drain do? It cordons the node as well, so no more pods can be scheduled on to the node.

Now we are ready to delete the node.

Removing nodes

The gke-kubectl-lab-default-pool-b3c7050d-8jhj node got drained and is not running any deployments, pods, or StatefulSets, so it can be easily deleted now.

We do it using the delete node command:

```
$ kubectl delete node gke-kubectl-lab-default-pool-b3c7050d-
8jhj
```

We delete the node using the preceding command. The output of this command is as shown in the following screenshot:

```
~ $ kubectl delete node gke-kubectl-lab-default-pool-b3c7050d-8jhj
node "gke-kubectl-lab-default-pool-b3c7050d-8jhj" deleted
~ $ kubectl get nodes
NAME                                          STATUS   ROLES    AGE    VERSION
gke-kubectl-lab-default-pool-b3c7050d-6s1l    Ready    <none>   3h7m   v1.17.5-gke.9
gke-kubectl-lab-default-pool-b3c7050d-d2lr    Ready    <none>   109m   v1.17.5-gke.9
```

Figure 3.12 – Delete node

As you can see from the `kubectl get nodes` output, the node was unregistered from the Kubernetes API and got deleted.

> **Important note**
>
> Actual node deletion depends on your Kubernetes setup. In cloud-hosted clusters, the node gets unregistered and deleted, but if you are running an on-premise self-hosted Kubernetes cluster, the actual node will not be deleted but only deregistered from the Kubernetes API.
>
> Also, when you specify the cluster size in the cloud setup, the new node will replace the deleted one after some time.

Let's run `kubectl get nodes` to check the nodes:

```
~ $ kubectl get nodes
NAME                                         STATUS   ROLES    AGE     VERSION
gke-kubectl-lab-default-pool-b3c7050d-6s1l   Ready    <none>   3h20m   v1.17.5-gke.9
gke-kubectl-lab-default-pool-b3c7050d-8jhj   Ready    <none>   82s     v1.17.5-gke.9
gke-kubectl-lab-default-pool-b3c7050d-d2lr   Ready    <none>   123m    v1.17.5-gke.9
```

Figure 3.13 – Nodes list

A few minutes later, we see the third node is back, even with the same name.

Introduction to node pools

Cloud providers that have Kubernetes as a managed service support node pools. Let's learn what they are.

A node pool is just a group of Kubernetes nodes that have the same compute spec and the same Kubernetes node labels, nothing else too fancy.

For example, we have two node pools:

- The default pool with the `node-pool: default-pool` node label
- The web app pool with the `node-pool: web-app` node label

Kubernetes node labels can be used in node selectors and Node Affinity to control how workloads are scheduled to your nodes.

We are going to learn how to use Kubernetes node pools with Node Affinity in *Chapter 5*, *Updating and Deleting Applications*.

Summary

In this chapter, we have learned how to use `kubectl` to list nodes running in the cluster, get information about the nodes and their resources usage; we've seen how to cordon, drain, and remove nodes; and we had an introduction to node pools.

We have learned new skills that can be applied in real-world scenarios to conduct maintenance on Kubernetes nodes.

In the next chapter, we're going to learn how to create and deploy applications to a Kubernetes cluster using `kubectl`.

Section 3: Application Management

This section explains how to manage Kubernetes applications, including creating, updating, deleting, viewing, and debugging applications.

This section contains the following chapters:

- *Chapter 4, Creating and Deploying Applications*
- *Chapter 5, Updating and Deleting Applications*
- *Chapter 6, Debugging an Application*

4

Creating and Deploying Applications

In the previous chapters, we have learned about Kubernetes nodes. Let's finally deploy an application using a Kubernetes deployment, scale the application up, and create a service for it.

A Kubernetes deployment is one way to deploy applications from Docker images, and we are going to use it for our example applications.

Kubernetes supports a few container runtimes, all of which can run Docker images:

- Docker
- CRI-O
- Containerd

In this chapter, we're going to cover the following topics:

- Introduction to pods
- Creating a deployment

- Creating a service
- Scaling up an application

Introduction to pods

A pod is a collocated group of application containers with shared volumes.

The applications in a pod all use the same network namespace, IP address, and port space. They can find and communicate with each other using localhost. Each pod has an IP address in a flat shared networking namespace that has full communication with other physical computers and containers across the network.

Pods are the smallest deployable units that can be created, scheduled, and managed with Kubernetes. Pods also can be created individually. As pods do not have a managed life cycle, if they die, they will not be recreated. For that reason, it is recommended that you use a deployment even if you are creating a single pod.

Pods are also used in DaemonSets, StatefulSets, Jobs, and CronJobs:

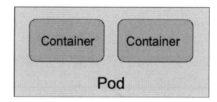

Figure 4.1 – Pod with two containers

The preceding diagram shows a pod with two containers. Containers in a pod share the same Linux network namespace as well as the following:

- IP address
- Localhost
- **IPC (inter-process communication)**

Let's move on to deployments, which are more suited to real-world application deployments.

Creating a deployment

The Kubernetes deployment provides updates for ReplicaSets, which ensures that a specified amount of pods (replicas) are running all the time:

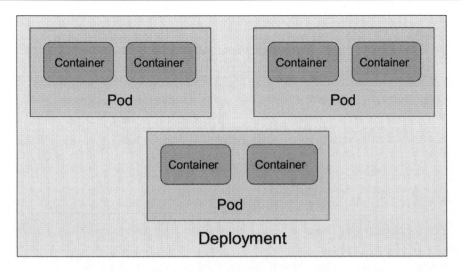

Figure 4.2 – Deployment with three pods

The preceding diagram shows a deployment with three pods; the ReplicaSet will try to keep three pods running all the time. Of course, if there are no free resources in the Kubernetes cluster, the running pod replicas might not match the required replica count.

There are a few ways to create a Kubernetes deployment – let's explore them. The easiest way is using $ kubectl create deployment.

Let's create an nginx deployment:

```
$ kubectl create deployment
deployment.apps/nginx created
```

Let's check the created nginx deployment:

```
$ kubectl get deployment
NAME     READY    UP-TO-DATE    AVAILABLE    AGE
nginx    1/1      1             1            19d
```

Let's check the created nginx pod:

```
$ kubectl get pods
NAME                     READY    STATUS    RESTARTS    AGE
nginx-86c57db685-c9s49   1/1      Running   0           10d
```

The preceding command created an nginx deployment with one nginx-86c57db685-c9s49 pod.

It looks almost too easy, right? One command and boom: your deployment is running.

> **Important note**
> The `kubectl create deployment` command is only recommended for testing images, as there you do not specify the deployment template and you do not have much control over any additional settings you might want to set for the deployment.

Let's deploy from the file using the `$ kubectl apply` command:

1. We have a file called `deployment.yaml` with the following contents:

```
$ cat deployment.yaml
apiVersion: apps/v1
kind: Deployment
metadata:
  name: nginx
  labels:
    app: nginx
spec:
  replicas: 1
  selector:
    matchLabels:
      app: nginx
  template:
    metadata:
      labels:
        app: nginx
    spec:
      containers:
      - image: nginx:1.18.0
        imagePullPolicy: IfNotPresent
        name: nginx
```

When using the preceding file with `kubectl`, it will deploy the same `nginx` deployment as we did using the `$ kubectl create deployment` command, but in this case, later on, we can update the file according to our needs and upgrade the deployment.

2. Let's delete the previously installed deployment:

```
$ kubectl delete deployment nginx
deployment.apps "nginx" deleted
```

3. Let's redeploy using the deployment.yaml file this time:

```
$ kubectl apply -f deployment.yaml
deployment.apps/nginx created
$ kubectl get deployment
NAME    READY    UP-TO-DATE    AVAILABLE    AGE
nginx   1/1      1                1           17s
$ kubectl get pods
NAME                    READY    STATUS    RESTARTS    AGE
nginx-7df9c6ff5-pnnr6   1/1      Running   0           25s
```

As you can see from the preceding commands, we have the deployment with one pod (replica) installed, but this time we used the template from the file.

The following diagram shows a deployment with three pods; the ReplicaSet will try to keep three pods uprunning at all times Again, if there are no free resources in the Kubernetes cluster, the running pod replicas might not match the required replica count:

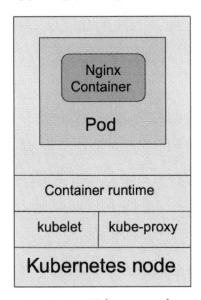

Figure 4.3 – Kubernetes node

Let's take a look at how to create a service.

Creating a service

Kubernetes services provide a single stable name and address for a set of pods. They act as basic in-cluster load balancers.

Most pods are designed to be long-running, but when a single process dies, the pod dies with it. If it dies, the Deployment replaces it with a new pod. Every pod gets its own dedicated IP address, which allows containers to have the same port (the exception is when NodePort is used), even if they're sharing the same host. But when a pod is started by the Deployment, the pod gets a new IP address.

This is where services really help. A service is attached to the deployment. Each service gets assigned a virtual IP address that remains constant until the service dies. As long as we know the service IP address, the service itself will keep track of the pods created by the deployment and will distribute requests to the deployment pods.

By setting the service, we get an internal Kubernetes DNS name. Also, the service acts as an in-cluster load balancer when you have more than one ReplicaSet. With a service, you can also expose your application to the internet when the service type is set to LoadBalancer:

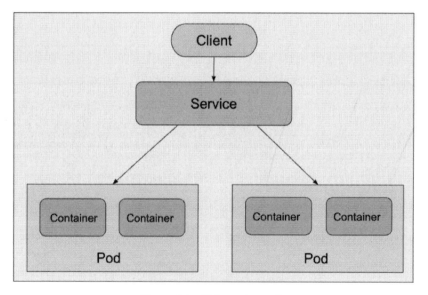

Figure 4.4 – Kubernetes node

The preceding diagram explains how a service works.

As we have our application up and running, let's create a Kubernetes service for it:

1. Let's start by running the following command:

```
$ kubectl expose deployment nginx --port=80 --target-port=80
service/nginx exposed
```

We used port 80, and on that port, the nginx service was exposed to other Kubernetes applications; target-port=80 is our nginx container port. We are using the port=80 container because the official nginx Docker image (https://hub.docker.com/_/nginx) we deployed in *Chapter 3, Working with Nodes*, uses port 80.

2. Let's check the created nginx service:

```
$ kubectl get service
NAME            TYPE         CLUSTER-IP      EXTERNAL-IP
PORT(S)
kubernetes      ClusterIP    10.16.0.1       <none>              443/
TCP
nginx           ClusterIP    10.16.12.233    <none>              80/
TCP
$ kubectl describe service nginx
Name:              nginx
Namespace:         default
Labels:            app=nginx
Annotations:       cloud.google.com/neg: {"ingress":true}
Selector:          app=nginx
Type:              ClusterIP
IP:                10.16.12.233
Port:              <unset>  80/TCP
TargetPort:        80/TCP
Endpoints:         10.8.0.133:80
Session Affinity:  None
Events:            <none>
```

The preceding kubectl get service command shows the services list and kubectl describe service nginx describes the service.

We can see a few things there:

- The service got the same name, nginx, as the deployment we exposed.
- Selector: app=nginx is the same as matchLabels in the nginx deployment; this is how the service knows how to connect to the right deployment.
- Type: ClusterIP is the default service type when no -type flag is provided.

> **Important note**
>
> Using the kubectl expose command looks like an easy way to set up a service for the application. But again, we cannot put that command under Git control, nor can we change the service settings. For testing purposes, this is fine, but not for running a real-world application.

Let's deploy from the file using the $ kubectl apply command.

We have a file called service.yaml that we are going to use to update the service:

```
$ cat service.yaml
apiVersion: v1
kind: Service
metadata:
  name: nginx
  labels:
    app: nginx
spec:
  type: ClusterIP
  ports:
  - port: 80
    protocol: TCP
    targetPort: 80
  selector:
    app: nginx
```

This time, let's keep the service we created with kubectl expose and see whether we can apply changes from the service.yaml file to the service we have created.

To deploy the service, we run the following command:

```
$ kubectl apply -f service.yaml
Warning: kubectl apply should be used on resource created by
ether kubectl create -save-config or kubetl apply
service/nginx configured
```

We got a warning (as first we used the kubectl expose command, and then we tried to update the service from the file), but our changes were applied to the service successfully, and from now on we can use service.yaml to make changes to the nginx service.

> **Tip**
>
> When you create a service with kubectl expose, you can export its template to the YAML file with the kubectl get service nginx -o yaml > service.yaml command and reuse the file for future changes that you might need to make.

To export the nginx service, run the following command:

```
$ kubectl get service nginx -o yaml
```

The output for the preceding command is as shown in the following screenshot:

```
code $ kubectl get service nginx -o yaml
apiVersion: v1
kind: Service
metadata:
  annotations:
    cloud.google.com/neg: '{"ingress":true}'
    kubectl.kubernetes.io/last-applied-configuration: |
      {"apiVersion":"v1","kind":"Service","metadata":{"annotations":{},"labels":{"app":"nginx
"},"name":"nginx","namespace":"default"},"spec":{"ports":[{"port":80,"protocol":"TCP","target
Port":80}],"selector":{"app":"nginx"},"type":"ClusterIP"}}
  creationTimestamp: "2020-07-03T13:40:27Z"
  labels:
    app: nginx
  name: nginx
  namespace: default
  resourceVersion: "12556354"
  selfLink: /api/v1/namespaces/default/services/nginx
  uid: 1702f08f-e63d-4b22-867f-c5c3f38bd569
spec:
  clusterIP: 10.16.7.200
  ports:
  - port: 80
    protocol: TCP
    targetPort: 80
  selector:
    app: nginx
  sessionAffinity: None
  type: ClusterIP
status:
  loadBalancer: {}
```

Figure 4.5 – Exporting the nginx service

Copy its contents to a file, and there you should remove the following parts, which were generated by `kubectl` and aren't needed there:

- `annotations`
- `creationTimestamp`
- `resourceVersion:`
- `selfLink`
- `uid`
- `Status`

> **Important note**
> You can also export a deployment's template to a YAML file using the `kubectl get deployment nginx -o yaml > deployment.yaml` command.

Scaling up an application

In the previous section, we deployed an application with one replica; let's scale its deployment to two replicas.

The use case of running multiple replicas is to enable high availability for an application. To scale our deployment, run the following commands:

```
$ kubectl scale deployment nginx --replicas=2
deployment.apps/nginx scaled
$ kubectl get deployment nginx
NAME      READY    UP-TO-DATE    AVAILABLE    AGE
nginx     2/2      2             2            5d17h
$ kubectl get pods
NAME                    READY    STATUS     RESTARTS    AGE
nginx-7df9c6ff5-chnrk   1/1      Running    0           29s
nginx-7df9c6ff5-s65dq   1/1      Running    0           5d17h
```

From the preceding output, we see can that the `$ kubectl get deployment nginx` command shows that the `nginx` deployment has two replicas. With `$ kubectl get pods`, we see two pods; one is just less than a minute old.

That's a neat command to scale deployments and is handy for testing purposes. Let's try to scale the deployment using the `deployment.yaml` file.

This time, let's scale to three replicas but using the `deployment.yaml` file:

1. Update `deployment.yaml` with three replicas:

   ```
   . . .
   spec:
     replicas: 3
   . . .
   ```

2. Run the same command as before:

   ```
   $ kubectl apply -f deployment.yaml
   deployment.apps/nginx configured
   $ kubectl get deployment nginx
   NAME      READY    UP-TO-DATE    AVAILABLE    AGE
   nginx     3/3      3             3            5d17h
   $ kubectl get pods
   NAME                    READY    STATUS     RESTARTS    AGE
   nginx-7df9c6ff5-chnrk   1/1      Running    0           21m
   nginx-7df9c6ff5-s65dq   1/1      Running    0
   5d17h
   nginx-7df9c6ff5-tk7g4   1/1      Running    0           22s
   ```

Nice: we have updated the `nginx` deployment with three replicas from the `deployment.yaml` file.

The service will distribute all incoming requests between the three pods in a round-robin manner.

Summary

In this chapter, we have learned how to create, deploy, and scale up applications with `kubectl`. The new skills we have learned in this chapter can now be used to deploy real-world applications.

In the next chapter, we going to learn how to do more advanced updates to deployed applications.

5

Updating and Deleting Applications

In the previous chapter, we learned how to deploy an application and its service and how to scale deployment replicas up. Let's now learn about some more advanced ways to update your application.

In this chapter, we're going to learn how to update applications to new versions and, if the release was a bad one, how to roll it back. We will see how to assign an application to a particular node, running applications in high-availability mode, how to make applications available over the internet, and in cases where there is a need, how to delete an application.

We're going to cover the following main topics in this chapter:

- Releasing a new application version
- Rolling back an application release
- Assigning an application to a specific node (node affinity)
- Scheduling application replicas to different nodes (pod affinity)

- Exposing an application to the internet

- Deleting an application

Deploying a new application version

In the previous chapter, we deployed an application using the `nginx v1.18.0` Docker image. In this section, let's update it to `nginx v1.19.0`:

To update the `nginx` Docker image tag, run the following command:

```
$ kubectl set image deployment nginx nginx=nginx:1.19.0 \
 --record
deployment.apps/nginx image updated
$ kubectl rollout status deployment nginx
deployment "nginx" successfully rolled out
$ kubectl get deployment nginx
NAME      READY   UP-TO-DATE   AVAILABLE   AGE
nginx     3/3     3            3           5d19h
$ kubectl get pods
NAME                    READY   STATUS    RESTARTS   AGE
nginx-6fd8f555b-2mktp   1/1     Running   0          60s
nginx-6fd8f555b-458cl   1/1     Running   0          62s
nginx-6fd8f555b-g728z   1/1     Running   0          66s
```

The `$ kubectl rollout status deployment nginx` command will show the rollout status as a success, failed, or waiting:

```
deployment "nginx" successfully rolled out
```

This is a handy way to check the deployment's rollout status.

Let's ensure that the deployment is updated to `nginx v1.19.0` by running the following command:

```
$ kubectl describe deployment nginx
```

The output for the preceding command can be seen in the following screenshot:

```
▶ code $ kubectl describe deployment nginx
Name:                    nginx
Namespace:               default
CreationTimestamp:       Sun, 28 Jun 2020 21:06:45 +0300
Labels:                  app=nginx
Annotations:             deployment.kubernetes.io/revision: 2
                         kubernetes.io/change-cause: kubectl set image deployment nginx nginx=nginx:1.19.0
Selector:                app=nginx
Replicas:                3 desired | 3 updated | 3 total | 3 available | 0 unavailable
StrategyType:            RollingUpdate
MinReadySeconds:         0
RollingUpdateStrategy:   25% max unavailable, 25% max surge
Pod Template:
  Labels:  app=nginx
  Containers:
   nginx:
    Image:        nginx:1.19.0
```

Figure 5.1 – Output for describe deployment

Yup, it was updated to v1.19.0, as we can see in the Pod Template part. Now, let's update the Docker image using the deployment.yaml file.

Update the deployment.yaml file with the new Docker image tag:

```
...
spec:
  containers:
  -image: nginx:1.19.0
...
```

Run the $ kubectl apply -f deployment.yaml command:

```
$ kubectl apply -f deployment.yaml
deployment.apps/nginx configured
$ kubectl rollout status deployment nginx
deployment "nginx" successfully rolled out
$ kubectl get deployment nginx
NAME      READY    UP-TO-DATE    AVAILABLE    AGE
nginx     3/3      3             3            5d19h
$ kubectl get pods
NAME                        READY    STATUS     RESTARTS    AGE
nginx-6fd8f555b-2mktp       1/1      Running    0           12m
nginx-6fd8f555b-458cl       1/1      Running    0           12m
nginx-6fd8f555b-g728z       1/1      Running    0           12m
```

Running the $ kubectl get pods command shows that the pods haven't changed as we applied the same Docker image tag as before, so Kubernetes is clever enough not to make any unnecessary changes to the nginx deployment.

Rolling back an application release

There are always cases (such as bugs in the code, the wrong Docker tag supplied for the latest release, and more) when you need to roll back an application release to a previous version.

This can be done using the $ kubectl rollout undo deployment nginx command followed by the get and describe commands:

```
▸ code $ kubectl rollout undo deployment nginx
deployment.apps/nginx rolled back
▸ code $ kubectl get pods
NAME                    READY   STATUS    RESTARTS   AGE
nginx-7df9bc6ff5-4kpbs  1/1     Running   0          48s
nginx-7df9bc6ff5-x7qbq  1/1     Running   0          50s
nginx-7df9bc6ff5-zfhmh  1/1     Running   0          47s
▸ code $ kubectl describe deployment nginx
Name:                   nginx
Namespace:              default
CreationTimestamp:      Sun, 28 Jun 2020 21:06:45 +0300
Labels:                 app=nginx
Annotations:            deployment.kubernetes.io/revision: 3
Selector:               app=nginx
Replicas:               3 desired | 3 updated | 3 total | 3 available | 0 unavailable
StrategyType:           RollingUpdate
MinReadySeconds:        0
RollingUpdateStrategy:  25% max unavailable, 25% max surge
Pod Template:
  Labels:  app=nginx
  Containers:
   nginx:
    Image:          nginx:1.18.0
```

Figure 5.2 – Deployment release rollback

The preceding output shows the version as Image: nginx:1.18.0, so the rollback was successful.

We can also check the deployment rollout history:

```
$ kubectl rollout history deployment nginx
deployment.apps/nginx
REVISION   CHANGE-CAUSE
1          <none>
2          <none>
```

We can also roll back to a specific revision:

```
$ kubectl rollout undo deployment nginx –to-revision=1
deployment.apps/nginx rolled back
```

Nice, we have learned how to roll back a deployment's release.

Assigning an application to a specific node (node affinity)

There are some use cases where Kubernetes clusters have different node pools with different specs, such as the following:

- Stateful applications
- Backend applications
- Frontend applications

Let's reschedule the `nginx` deployment to a dedicated node pool:

1. To get the nodes list, run the following command:

   ```
   $ kubectl get nodes
   ```

   The preceding command gives the following output:

   ```
   ▶ code $ kubectl get nodes
   NAME                                         STATUS   ROLES    AGE     VERSION
   gke-kubectl-lab-default-pool-b3c7050d-2811   Ready    <none>   26h     v1.17.5-gke.9
   gke-kubectl-lab-default-pool-b3c7050d-2sxq   Ready    <none>   140m    v1.17.5-gke.9
   gke-kubectl-lab-default-pool-b3c7050d-5w59   Ready    <none>   26h     v1.17.5-gke.9
   gke-kubectl-lab-we-app-pool-1302ab74-czpl    Ready    <none>   3m18s   v1.17.6-gke.7
   gke-kubectl-lab-we-app-pool-1302ab74-lh7j    Ready    <none>   3m18s   v1.17.6-gke.7
   gke-kubectl-lab-we-app-pool-1302ab74-pg34    Ready    <none>   3m19s   v1.17.6-gke.7
   ```

   Figure 5.3 – Node pools list

2. Next, let's check a node under the `gke-kubectl-lab-we-app-pool` name. Run the following command:

   ```
   $ kubectl describe node gke-kubectl-lab-we-app-pool-
   1302ab74-pg34
   ```

The output of the preceding command is as shown in the following screenshot:

```
▶ code $ kubectl describe node gke-kubectl-lab-we-app-pool-1302ab74-pg34
Name:                    gke-kubectl-lab-we-app-pool-1302ab74-pg34
Roles:                   <none>
Labels:                  beta.kubernetes.io/arch=amd64
                         beta.kubernetes.io/instance-type=n1-standard-1
                         beta.kubernetes.io/os=linux
                         cloud.google.com/gke-nodepool=we-app-pool
                         cloud.google.com/gke-os-distribution=cos
                         cloud.google.com/gke-preemptible=true
                         failure-domain.beta.kubernetes.io/region=us-central1
                         failure-domain.beta.kubernetes.io/zone=us-central1-c
                         kubernetes.io/arch=amd64
                         kubernetes.io/hostname=gke-kubectl-lab-we-app-pool-1302ab74-pg34
                         kubernetes.io/os=linux
                         node-pool=web-app
                         node.kubernetes.io/instance-type=n1-standard-1
                         topology.kubernetes.io/region=us-central1
                         topology.kubernetes.io/zone=us-central1-c
```

Figure 5.4 – Node labels

3. There, we have a `node-pool=web-app` label, which is the same for all nodes of the `gke-kubectl-lab-we-app-pool` pool.

4. Let's update the `deployment.yaml` file with the `nodeAffinity` rule, so the `nginx` application only gets scheduled to `gke-kubectl-lab-we-app-pool`:

```
    ...
    spec:
      affinity:
        nodeAffinity:
          requiredDuringSchedulingIgnoredDuringExecution:
            nodeSelectorTerms:
            - matchExpressions:
              - key: node-pool
                operator: In
                values:
                - "web-app"
      containers:
    ...
```

5. To deploy the changes, run the `$ kubectl apply -f deployment.yaml` command followed by the `get` command as shown in the following screenshot:

```
> code $ kubectl apply -f deployment.yaml
deployment.apps/nginx configured
> code $ kubectl get pods -o wide
NAME                    READY   STATUS    RESTARTS   AGE   IP           NODE
nginx-55b7cd4f4b-nt926  1/1     Running   0          44s   10.8.1.130   gke-kubectl-lab-we-app-pool-1302ab74-lh7j
nginx-55b7cd4f4b-rdpm8  1/1     Running   0          62s   10.8.2.2     gke-kubectl-lab-we-app-pool-1302ab74-czpl
nginx-55b7cd4f4b-tnmpx  1/1     Running   0          54s   10.8.2.130   gke-kubectl-lab-we-app-pool-1302ab74-pg34
```

Figure 5.5 – Node affinity

Nice, the pods were scheduled onto `gke-kubectl-lab-we-app-pool`.

> **Tip**
>
> We have used the `-o wide` flag, which allows us to show more information about a pod, such as its IP and the node it's scheduled on.

6. Let's delete one pod to verify that it gets scheduled onto `gke-kubectl-lab-we-app-pool`:

```
$ kubectl delete pod nginx-55b7cd4f4b-tnmpx
```

Let's get the pods list again:

```
> code $ kubectl get pods -o wide
NAME                    READY   STATUS    RESTARTS   AGE    IP           NODE
nginx-55b7cd4f4b-mdh6b  1/1     Running   0          6s     10.8.2.131   gke-kubectl-lab-we-app-pool-1302ab74-pg34
nginx-55b7cd4f4b-nt926  1/1     Running   0          7m43s  10.8.1.130   gke-kubectl-lab-we-app-pool-1302ab74-lh7j
nginx-55b7cd4f4b-rdpm8  1/1     Running   0          8m1s   10.8.2.2     gke-kubectl-lab-we-app-pool-1302ab74-czpl
```

Figure 5.6 – Pods list with nodes

The preceding screenshot shows the pods list with the nodes the pods were scheduled on. Good, the new pod was scheduled onto the right node pool.

Scheduling application replicas to different nodes (pod affinity)

Using `nodeAffinity` does not ensure that pods will next time be scheduled onto separate nodes, and for real application high availability, the best practice is to ensure that application pods are scheduled onto separate nodes. If one of the nodes is down/rebooted/replaced, having all the pods running on that node will cause the application to go down and its services to be unavailable.

Let's update the `deployment.yaml` file with the `podAntiAffinity` rule so that the `nginx` application is only scheduled to `gke-kubectl-lab-we-app-pool` and onto separate nodes:

```
...
spec:
  affinity:
    nodeAffinity:
      requiredDuringSchedulingIgnoredDuringExecution:
        nodeSelectorTerms:
        - matchExpressions:
          - key: node-pool
            operator: In
            values:
            - "web-app"
    podAntiAffinity:
      requiredDuringSchedulingIgnoredDuringExecution:
      - labelSelector:
          matchExpressions:
          - key: app
            operator: In
            values:
            - nginx
        topologyKey: "kubernetes.io/hostname"
  containers:
...
```

To deploy the new changes, run the `$ kubectl apply -f deployment.yaml` command followed by the `get` command as shown in the following screenshot:

```
▶ code $ kubectl apply -f deployment.yaml
deployment.apps/nginx configured
▶ code $ kubectl get pods -o wide
NAME                       READY   STATUS             RESTARTS   AGE   IP           NODE
nginx-55b7cd4f4b-fm7fl     0/1     Terminating        0          80s   10.8.2.3     gke-kubectl-lab-we-app-pool-1302ab74-czpl
nginx-55b7cd4f4b-rdpm8     1/1     Running            0          63m   10.8.2.2     gke-kubectl-lab-we-app-pool-1302ab74-czpl
nginx-754bdfd944-6lmvz     1/1     Running            0          4s    10.8.2.133   gke-kubectl-lab-we-app-pool-1302ab74-pg34
nginx-754bdfd944-7km99     1/1     Running            0          5s    10.8.3.3     gke-kubectl-lab-we-app-pool-1302ab74-mvqs
nginx-754bdfd944-kflzn     0/1     ContainerCreating  0          2s    <none>       gke-kubectl-lab-we-app-pool-1302ab74-lh7j
```

Figure 5.7 – Node affinity

As you can see, the pods are rescheduled again as we added the `podAntiAffinity` rule:

```
code $ kubectl get pods -o wide
NAME                     READY   STATUS    RESTARTS   AGE   IP           NODE
nginx-754bdfd944-6lmvz   1/1     Running   0          22s   10.8.2.133   gke-kubectl-lab-we-app-pool-1302ab74-pg34
nginx-754bdfd944-7km99   1/1     Running   0          23s   10.8.3.3     gke-kubectl-lab-we-app-pool-1302ab74-mvqs
nginx-754bdfd944-kflzn   1/1     Running   0          20s   10.8.1.132   gke-kubectl-lab-we-app-pool-1302ab74-lh7j
```

Figure 5.8 – Node affinity pods are rescheduled

As you can see, the pods are running on separate nodes, and the `podAntiAffinity` rule will ensure that pods will not be scheduled onto the same node.

Exposing an application to the internet

Awesome job so far, so to finish this chapter, let's make our application available over the internet.

We need to update `service.yaml` with `type: LoadBalancer`, which will create a LoadBalancer with an external IP.

> **Note**
> The LoadBalancer capability is dependent on the vendor integration because an external LoadBalancer is created by the vendor. So, if you run locally with Minikube or Kind, you will never really get an external IP.

Update the `service.yaml` file with the following content:

```
...
spec:
  type: LoadBalancer
...
```

To deploy the new changes, run the `$ kubectl apply -f service.yaml` command followed by the `get` command as shown in the following screenshot:

```
code $ kubectl apply -f service.yaml
service/nginx configured
code $ kubectl get service
NAME         TYPE           CLUSTER-IP    EXTERNAL-IP   PORT(S)        AGE
kubernetes   ClusterIP      10.16.0.1     <none>        443/TCP        28d
nginx        LoadBalancer   10.16.7.200   <pending>     80:31212/TCP   27h
```

Figure 5.9 – Service with pending LoadBalancer

We are seeing `pending` as the status depends on the cloud provider, and it can take up to 5 minutes for the LoadBalancer to be provisioned. Running the `get` command again after some time, you can see that the IP is assigned, as shown in the following screenshot:

```
▶ code $ kubectl get service
NAME          TYPE           CLUSTER-IP     EXTERNAL-IP       PORT(S)        AGE
kubernetes    ClusterIP      10.16.0.1      <none>            443/TCP        28d
nginx         LoadBalancer   10.16.7.200    104.197.177.53    80:31212/TCP   27h
```

Figure 5.10 – The service with LoadBalancer

To be sure that the application is working, let's open IP `104.197.177.53` in the browser:

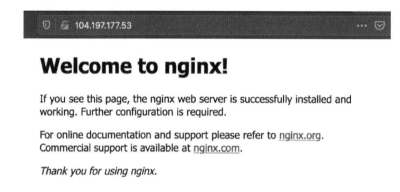

Figure 5.11 – Application in the browser

Voila! Our application is accessible from the internet.

> **Important note**
> The preceding example showing how to expose the application to the internet is not secure, as it is using HTTP. To keep the example simple, we used HTTP, but real-world applications should use HTTPS only.

Deleting an application

Sometimes, you need to delete an application, so let's go over a few options for how to do that.

In the previous sections, we deployed the deployment and service. Let's refresh our memory on what we deployed.

To check the deployments, run the following command:

```
$ kubectl get deployment
NAME      READY    UP-TO-DATE    AVAILABLE    AGE
nginx     3/3      3             3            6d17h
```

To check the active services, run the following command:

```
$ kubectl get service
NAME         TYPE          CLUSTER-IP     EXTERNAL-IP       PORT(S)
kubernetes   ClusterIP     10.16.0.1      <none>            443/TCP
nginx        LoadBalancer  10.16.12.134   104.197.177.53
80:30295/TCP
```

We have a deployment called `nginx` and a service called `nginx`.

First, let's delete the `nginx` service using the following command:

```
$ kubectl delete service nginx
service "nginx" deleted
$ kubectl get service
NAME         TYPE          CLUSTER-IP     EXTERNAL-IP       PORT(S)
kubernetes   ClusterIP     10.16.0.1      <none>            443/TCP
```

As you can see in the preceding screenshot, the `nginx` service was deleted, and the application is not exposed to the internet anymore and is safe to be deleted as well. To delete the `nginx` deployment, run the following command:

```
$ kubectl delete deployment nginx
deployment.apps "nginx" deleted
$ kubectl get deployment
No resources found in default namespace.
```

It is so easy to delete an application's deployed resources with a few commands.

But if you have an image where you have more than just two resources installed, would you run a deletion command for each resource? Of course not, there is an easier way to do that.

As we have deleted the deployment and service, let's deploy them again so that we have something to delete again. You need to put `deployment.yaml` and `service.yaml` into some folder – for example, `code`.

This will allow you to manage multiple resources together as multiple files in a directory.

> **Note**
>
> You can also have multiple YAML entries in a single YAML file (with the - - - divider).

To install the deployment and service with the same command, run the following command:

```
$ kubectl apply -f code/
deployment.apps/nginx created
service/nginx created
```

To check the deployment and service, run the following commands:

```
$ kubectl get deployment
NAME     READY   UP-TO-DATE   AVAILABLE   AGE
nginx    3/3     3            3           13s
$ kubectl get service
NAME         TYPE           CLUSTER-IP    EXTERNAL-IP   PORT(S)
kubernetes   ClusterIP      10.16.0.1     <none>        443/TCP
nginx        LoadBalancer   10.16.4.143   pending
80:32517/TCP
```

This time, we used one command to install the application, and in the same way, you can apply changes to the application as well, as Kubernetes is clever enough that it will only update the resource that was changed.

> **Note**
>
> You can also use one command to show a service and deployment:
> `kubectl get deployment/service`.

We can also use the same approach to delete the application. To delete the deployment and service with one command, run the following:

```
$ kubectl delete -f code/
deployment.apps/nginx deleted
service/nginx deleted
$ kubectl get deployment
```

```
No resources found in default namespace.
$ kubectl get service
NAME          TYPE        CLUSTER-IP     EXTERNAL-IP     PORT(S)
kubernetes    ClusterIP   10.16.0.1      <none>          443/TCP
```

As you can see, we used just one command to clean up all of the application's installed resources.

Summary

In this chapter, we learned how to release a new application version, roll back an application version, assign an application to a particular node, schedule application replicas between different nodes, and expose an application to the internet. We also learned how to delete an application in a few different ways.

In the next chapter, we are going to learn how to debug an application, which is really important to know as it is not always the case that an application's releases go well.

6
Debugging an Application

There are times when you need to debug an application to troubleshoot production-related issues. So far in this book, we have learned how to install, update, and delete an application.

In this chapter, we are going to cover application debugging by using `kubectl describe` to show the resolved object configuration and desired state before the actual events in the pod. Then we are going to check pod logs for errors, and finally, executing in a container (executing into a container means getting shell access in the running container) and running a command there.

In this chapter, we're going to cover the following main topics:

- Describing a pod
- Checking pod logs
- Executing a command in a running container

Describing a pod

In the previous chapter, we deleted a running application. For this chapter, then, let's install another one. For the purpose of debugging an application, we are going to use the bitnami/postgresql Docker image from Docker Hub (https://hub.docker. com/r/bitnami/postgresql) and we are going to install an application using the deployment-postgresql.yaml file:

```
$ cat deployment-postgresql.yaml
apiVersion: apps/v1
kind: Deployment
metadata:
  name: postgresql
  labels:
    app: postgresql
spec:
  replicas: 1
  selector:
    matchLabels:
      app: postgresql
  template:
    metadata:
      labels:
        app: postgresql
    spec:
      containers:
      - image: bitnami/postgresql:10.12.10
        imagePullPolicy: IfNotPresent
        name: postgresql
```

To install the PostgreSQL deployment, run the following commands:

```
$ kubectl apply -f deployment-postgresql.yaml
Deployment.apps/postgresql created
$ kubectl get pods
NAME                          READY   STATUS      RESTARTS   AGE
postgresql-867df7d69-r84nl    0/1     ErrImagePull   0            9s
```

Oops, what happened there? By running the $ kubectl get pods command we are seeing an ErrImagePull error. Let's look into it. In *Chapter 1*, *Introducing and Installing kubectl*, we learned about the kubectl describe command; let's use it to check the pod status. To describe the PostgreSQL pod, run the following command:

```
$ kubectl describe pod postgresql-8675df7d69-r84nl
```

We get the following output of Events after running the preceding command:

```
Events:
  Type      Reason      Age                     From
  Message
  ----      ------      ----                    ----
  -------
  Normal    Scheduled   12m                     default-scheduler
  Successfully assigned default/postgresql-8675df7d69-r84nl to gke-kubectl-lab-default-pool-b3c70
  50d-httc
  Normal    Pulling     11m (x4 over 12m)       kubelet, gke-kubectl-lab-default-pool-b3c7050d-httc
  Pulling image "bitnami/postgresql:10.12.10"
  Warning   Failed      11m (x4 over 12m)       kubelet, gke-kubectl-lab-default-pool-b3c7050d-httc
  Failed to pull image "bitnami/postgresql:10.12.10": rpc error: code = Unknown desc = Error resp
  onse from daemon: manifest for bitnami/postgresql:10.12.10 not found: manifest unknown: manifest
  unknown
  Warning   Failed      11m (x4 over 12m)       kubelet, gke-kubectl-lab-default-pool-b3c7050d-httc
  Error: ErrImagePull
  Normal    BackOff     10m (x6 over 12m)       kubelet, gke-kubectl-lab-default-pool-b3c7050d-httc
  Back-off pulling image "bitnami/postgresql:10.12.10"
  Warning   Failed      2m34s (x43 over 12m)  kubelet, gke-kubectl-lab-default-pool-b3c7050d-httc
  Error: ImagePullBackOff
```

Figure 6.1 – The output for the describe command

In the preceding screenshot, as the output of kubectl pod describe is quite big, we are only showing the Events part, which we need to check to troubleshoot the issue.

Right here, we see why it fails to pull the image:

```
Failed to pull image "bitnami/postgresql:10.12.10": rpc error:
code = Unknown desc = Error response from daemon: manifest
for bitnami/postgresql:10.12.10 not found: manifest unknown:
manifest unknown
```

Looking at the preceding error, we can see that we have referenced the wrong tag for the postgresql Docker image. Let's change it to 10.13.0 in the deployment-postgresql.yaml file and run kubectl apply again. To update the postgresql deployment, run the following commands:

```
$ kubectl apply -f deployment-postgresql.yaml
Deployment.apps/postgresql configured
$ kubectl get pods
```

NAME AGE	READY	STATUS	RESTARTS
postgresql-56dcb95567-8rdmd 36s	0/1	CrashLoopBackOff	0
postgresql-8675df7d69-r84nl 35m	0/1	ImagePullBackOff	0

We are seeing a new pod, postgresql-56dcb95567-8rdmd, which is crashing too. To check this postgresql pod, run the following command:

```
$ kubectl describe pod postgresql-56dcb95567-8rdmd
```

We get the following output after running the preceding command:

```
Events:
  Type     Reason     Age                   From
  Message
  ----     ------     ----                  ----
  -------
  Normal   Scheduled  7m36s                 default-scheduler
  Successfully assigned default/postgresql-56dcb95567-8rdmd to gke-kubectl-lab-default-pool-b3c7050
  d-httc
  Normal   Pulled     6m13s (x5 over 7m35s)  kubelet, gke-kubectl-lab-default-pool-b3c7050d-httc
  Container image "bitnami/postgresql:10.13.0" already present on machine
  Normal   Created    6m13s (x5 over 7m35s)  kubelet, gke-kubectl-lab-default-pool-b3c7050d-httc
  Created container postgresql
  Normal   Started    6m13s (x5 over 7m35s)  kubelet, gke-kubectl-lab-default-pool-b3c7050d-httc
  Started container postgresql
  Warning  BackOff    2m23s (x26 over 7m33s) kubelet, gke-kubectl-lab-default-pool-b3c7050d-httc
  Back-off restarting failed container
```

Figure 6.2 – Checking the postgresql pod with fixed Docker tag

Hmm, this time, Events does not list much information as to why the postgresql pod is in the CrashLoopBackOff state, as the bitnami/postgresql:10.13.0 image was pulled successfully.

Let's learn what to do about this issue in the next section by checking the pod's logs.

Checking pod logs

When kubectl describe pod does not show any information about an error, we can use another kubectl command, that is, logs. The kubectl logs command allows us to print container logs, and we can also view them in real time as well.

> **Tip**
>
> You can use `kubectl logs` with a flag to print the logs for the previous instance of the container in a pod if it exists:
>
> ```
> $ kubectl logs -p some_pod
> ```

Now, let's check out this command on the crashing `postgresql` pod and try to find out what is going on with it – why it is failing. To get the pods list and check the pod logs, run the following commands:

```
$ kubectl get pods
```

```
$ kubectl logs postgresql-56dcb95567-njsp6
```

The output for the preceding commands is shown in the following screenshot:

```
> code $ kubectl get pods
NAME                          READY   STATUS            RESTARTS   AGE
postgresql-56dcb95567-njsp6   0/1     CrashLoopBackOff  7          5d20h
> code $ kubectl logs postgresql-56dcb95567-njsp6
postgresql 12:44:13.15
postgresql 12:44:13.15 Welcome to the Bitnami postgresql container
postgresql 12:44:13.15 Subscribe to project updates by watching https://github.com/bitnami/bitnami-docker-postgres
ql
postgresql 12:44:13.16 Submit issues and feature requests at https://github.com/bitnami/bitnami-docker-postgresql/
issues
postgresql 12:44:13.16
postgresql 12:44:13.17 INFO  ==> ** Starting PostgreSQL setup **
postgresql 12:44:13.18 INFO  ==> Validating settings in POSTGRESQL_* env vars..
postgresql 12:44:13.19 ERROR ==> The POSTGRESQL_PASSWORD environment variable is empty or not set. Set the environ
ment variable ALLOW_EMPTY_PASSWORD=yes to allow the container to be started with blank passwords. This is recommen
ded only for development.
postgresql 12:44:13.19 ERROR ==> The POSTGRESQL_PASSWORD environment variable is empty or not set. Set the environ
ment variable ALLOW_EMPTY_PASSWORD=yes to allow the container to be started with blank passwords. This is recommen
ded only for development.
```

Figure 6.3 – Getting error logs for the postgresql pod

Aha! As you can see from the preceding screenshot, the `postgresql` pod is failing as it needs the `POSTGRESQL_PASSWORD` environment variable to be set with some password, or the `ALLOW_EMPTY_PASSWORD` environment variable set to `yes`, which will allow the container to be started with the blank password.

Let's update the `deployment-postgresql.yaml` file with the `POSTGRESQL_PASSWORD` environment variable set with some password:

```
$ cat deployment-postgresql.yaml
apiVersion: apps/v1
kind: Deployment
metadata:
  name: postgresql
```

```
  labels:
    app: postgresql
spec:
  replicas: 1
  selector:
    matchLabels:
      app: postgresql
  template:
    metadata:
      labels:
        app: postgresql
    spec:
      containers:
      - image: bitnami/postgresql:10.13.0
        imagePullPolicy: IfNotPresent
        name: postgresql
        env:
        - name: POSTGRESQL_PASSWORD
          value: "VerySecurePassword:-)"
```

To update the postgresql deployment, run the following commands:

```
$ kubectl apply -f deployment-postgresql.yaml
Deployment.apps/postgresql configured
$ kubectl get pods
```

NAME AGE	READY	STATUS	RESTARTS
postgresql-56dcb95567-njsp6 36m	0/1	CrashLoopBackOff	11
postgresql-57578b68d9-b6lkv 1s	0/1	ContainerCreating 0	

```
$ kubectl get pods
```

NAME	READY	STATUS	RESTARTS	AGE
postgresql-57578b68d9-b6lkv	1/1	Running	0	21s

As you can see in the preceding code block, the `postgresql` deployment was updated, a new pod was created successfully, and the pod that was crashing has been terminated.

> **Important note**
>
> Best practices do not recommend storing passwords directly in deployments and other Kubernetes templates, but storing them in Kubernetes Secrets instead.

Now let's see what the `postgresql` pod logs show in real time. To check the pod logs in real time, run the following command:

```
$ kubectl logs postgresql-57578b68d9-b6lkv -f
```

The output of the preceding command is shown in the following screenshot:

```
▸ code $ kubectl logs postgresql-57578b68d9-b6lkv -f
postgresql 13:03:29.35
postgresql 13:03:29.35 Welcome to the Bitnami postgresql container
postgresql 13:03:29.35 Subscribe to project updates by watching https://github.com/bitnami/bitnami-docker-postgres
ql
postgresql 13:03:29.36 Submit issues and feature requests at https://github.com/bitnami/bitnami-docker-postgresql/
issues
postgresql 13:03:29.36
postgresql 13:03:29.39 INFO  ==> ** Starting PostgreSQL setup **
postgresql 13:03:29.41 INFO  ==> Validating settings in POSTGRESQL_* env vars..
postgresql 13:03:29.42 INFO  ==> Loading custom pre-init scripts...
postgresql 13:03:29.42 INFO  ==> Initializing PostgreSQL database...
postgresql 13:03:29.44 INFO  ==> pg_hba.conf file not detected. Generating it...
postgresql 13:03:29.44 INFO  ==> Generating local authentication configuration
postgresql 13:03:31.23 INFO  ==> Starting PostgreSQL in background...
postgresql 13:03:31.36 INFO  ==> Changing password of postgres
postgresql 13:03:31.38 INFO  ==> Configuring replication parameters
postgresql 13:03:31.40 INFO  ==> Configuring fsync
postgresql 13:03:31.40 INFO  ==> Loading custom scripts...
postgresql 13:03:31.41 INFO  ==> Enabling remote connections
postgresql 13:03:31.42 INFO  ==> Stopping PostgreSQL...
postgresql 13:03:32.43 INFO  ==> ** PostgreSQL setup finished! **

postgresql 13:03:32.45 INFO  ==> ** Starting PostgreSQL **
2020-07-18 13:03:32.468 GMT [1] LOG:  listening on IPv4 address "0.0.0.0", port 5432
2020-07-18 13:03:32.468 GMT [1] LOG:  listening on IPv6 address "::", port 5432
2020-07-18 13:03:32.473 GMT [1] LOG:  listening on Unix socket "/tmp/.s.PGSQL.5432"
2020-07-18 13:03:32.487 GMT [105] LOG:  database system was shut down at 2020-07-18 13:03:31 GMT
2020-07-18 13:03:32.493 GMT [1] LOG:  database system is ready to accept connections
```

Figure 6.4 – Reviewing the logs for postgresql

Nice, the PostgreSQL deployment is up and running and is ready to accept connections. By leaving that command running, we can review the logs in real time when we need to see what is going on in the PostgreSQL container.

Executing a command in a running container

So, we have learned how to troubleshoot pods with `pod describe` and `logs`, but there might be some cases when you want to do even more advanced troubleshooting, such as checking some config files or running some commands in the container. These things can be done using the `kubectl exec` command, which will allow `exec` into the container and have an interactive session in the container or run your commands as well.

Let's see how to get the `postgresql.conf` file content using the `kubectl exec` command:

```
$ kubectl exec postgresql-57578b68d9-6wvpw cat \ /opt/bitnami/
postgresql/conf/postgresql.conf
# ------------------------------
# PostgreSQL configuration file
# ------------------------------
#
# This file consists of lines of the form:
#
#    name = value
#
# (The "=" is optional.)  Whitespace may be used.  Comments are
introduced with
# "#" anywhere on a line.  The complete list of parameter names
and allowed
# values can be found in the PostgreSQL documentation.
...
```

The preceding command will show the `postgresql.conf` file content so you can check the PostgreSQL settings, which in this case, are set by default.

Next, let's `exec` into the `postgresql` pod, open a shell, and then run the `psql` command to check for available databases.

To execute into the `postgresql` pod please run the following command:

```
$ kubectl exec -it postgresql-57578b68d9-6wvpw - bash
```

The output for the preceding command is shown in the following screenshot:

```
▶ code $ kubectl exec -it postgresql-57578b68d9-6wvpw -- bash
I have no name!@postgresql-57578b68d9-6wvpw:/$ psql -Upostgres
Password for user postgres:
psql (10.13)
Type "help" for help.

postgres=# \l
                                 List of databases
    Name    |  Owner   | Encoding |  Collate    |   Ctype     |   Access privileges
------------+----------+----------+-------------+-------------+-----------------------
 postgres   | postgres | UTF8     | en_US.UTF-8 | en_US.UTF-8 |
 template0  | postgres | UTF8     | en_US.UTF-8 | en_US.UTF-8 | =c/postgres         +
            |          |          |             |             | postgres=CTc/postgres
 template1  | postgres | UTF8     | en_US.UTF-8 | en_US.UTF-8 | =c/postgres         +
            |          |          |             |             | postgres=CTc/postgres
(3 rows)
```

Figure 6.5 – Execute into the postgresql pod

As you see in the preceding screenshot, we used `exec` to get into the `postgresql` pod using the `bash` shell, then we ran `psql -Upostgres` to log in to the `postgresql` instance, before checking for available databases with `\l`. This is a nice example of how to use the interactive `exec` command and run different commands inside of a container.

Summary

In this chapter, we learned how to describe the pod, check logs, and troubleshoot issues, and also covered how to create a Kubernetes deployment from scratch for the `postgresql` Docker image.

The troubleshooting skills of using `kubectl describe`, `logs`, and `exec` are very useful and allow you to know what is happening in an application pod. These techniques can be used to help you to fix any issues you encounter.

In the next chapter, we're going to learn how to extend `kubectl` with plugins.

Section 4: Extending kubectl

This section explains how to manage Kubernetes plugins, shows how to use Kustomize and Helm, and covers commands for Docker users.

This section contains the following chapters:

- *Chapter 7, Working with kubectl Plugins*
- *Chapter 8, Introducing Kustomize for Kubernetes*
- *Chapter 9, Introducing Helm for Kubernetes*
- *Chapter 10, kubectl Best Practices and Docker Commands*

7

Working with kubectl Plugins

In the previous chapter, we learned how to do various operations with `kubectl`, such as listing nodes and pods and checking logs. In this chapter, let's learn how to extend the `kubectl` command base with plugins. `kubectl` has many commands but might not always have the ones you want, and, in such instances, we need to use plugins. We will learn how to install `kubectl` plugins in order to have more features with extra sub-commands. We will see how to use those plugins, and finally, we will see how we can create a basic plugin for `kubectl`.

In this chapter, we're going to cover the following main topics:

- Installing plugins
- Using plugins
- Creating basic plugin

Installing plugins

A plugin in `kubectl` is just an executable file (it could be a complied Go program or a Bash shell script, among other things) the name of which begins with `kubectl-`, and to install the plugin you just have to put its executable file in a directory that's in your `PATH` variable.

The easiest way to find and install plugins is by using **Krew** (https://krew.sigs.k8s. io/), the Kubernetes plugin manager. Krew is available for macOS, Linux, and Windows.

Krew is a Kubernetes plugin, so let's go ahead and install it. For this example, we are going to use macOS:

1. To install Krew on macOS, run the $ brew install krew command as shown in the following screenshot:

```
▸ code $ brew install krew
Updating Homebrew...
  ═══▶ Downloading https://homebrew.bintray.com/bottles/krew-0.3.4.catalina.bottle.tar.gz
Already downloaded: /Users/rimasm/Library/Caches/Homebrew/downloads/f1bdab052a4e7f8be0
7a7c3060f9d45c--krew-0.3.4.catalina.bottle.tar.gz
  ═══▶ Pouring krew-0.3.4.catalina.bottle.tar.gz
  🍺  /usr/local/Cellar/krew/0.3.4: 5 files, 11.3MB
```

Figure 7.1 – krew install with brew on macOS

2. Next, we need to download the plugin list:

```
$ kubectl krew update
```

3. When we have a locally cached list of all the plugins, let's check for available plugins by running the $ kubectl krew search command as shown in the following screenshot:

```
▸ code $ kubectl krew search
NAME                DESCRIPTION                                     INSTALLED
access-matrix       Show an RBAC access matrix for server resources no
advise-psp          Suggests PodSecurityPolicies for cluster.       no
apparmor-manager    Manage AppArmor profiles for cluster.           no
auth-proxy          Authentication proxy to a pod or service        no
bulk-action         Do bulk actions on Kubernetes resources.        no
ca-cert             Print the PEM CA certificate of the current clu... no
capture             Triggers a Sysdig capture to troubleshoot the r... no
cert-manager        Manage cert-manager resources inside your cluster no
change-ns           View or change the current namespace via kubectl. no
cilium              Easily interact with Cilium agents.             no
cluster-group       Exec commands across a group of contexts.       no
config-cleanup      Automatically clean up your kubeconfig          no
cssh                SSH into Kubernetes nodes                       no
ctx                 Switch between contexts in your kubeconfig      no
custom-cols         A "kubectl get" replacement with customizable c... no
debug               Attach ephemeral debug container to running pod no
debug-shell         Create pod with interactive kube-shell          no
deprecations        Checks for deprecated objects in a cluster      no
df-pv               Show disk usage (like unix df) for persistent v... no
doctor              Scans your cluster and reports anomalies.       no
duck                List custom resources with ducktype support     no
eksporter           Export resources and removes a pre-defined set ... no
evict-pod           Evicts the given pod                            no
```

Figure 7.2 – List of available plugins

As the list has more than 90 plugins, in the preceding screenshot we are just showing only part of the list.

4. Let's install a few handy plugins to expand the `kubectl` command base by running the `$ kubectl krew install ctx ns view-allocations` command as shown in the following screenshot:

```
▶ code $ kubectl krew install ctx ns view-allocations
Updated the local copy of plugin index.
Installing plugin: ctx
Installed plugin: ctx
\
 | Use this plugin:
 |       kubectl ctx
 | Documentation:
 |       https://github.com/ahmetb/kubectx
 | Caveats:
 | \
 |  | If fzf is installed on your machine, you can interactively choose
 |  | between the entries using the arrow keys, or by fuzzy searching
 |  | as you type.
 |  | See https://github.com/ahmetb/kubectx for customization and details.
 | /
/
WARNING: You installed plugin "ctx" from the krew-index plugin repository.
    These plugins are not audited for security by the Krew maintainers.
    Run them at your own risk.
Installing plugin: ns
Installed plugin: ns
\
 | Use this plugin:
 |       kubectl ns
 | Documentation:
 |       https://github.com/ahmetb/kubectx
 | Caveats:
 | \
 |  | If fzf is installed on your machine, you can interactively choose
 |  | between the entries using the arrow keys, or by fuzzy searching
 |  | as you type.
 | /
/
WARNING: You installed plugin "ns" from the krew-index plugin repository.
    These plugins are not audited for security by the Krew maintainers.
    Run them at your own risk.
Installing plugin: view-allocations
Installed plugin: view-allocations
\
 | Use this plugin:
 |       kubectl view-allocations
 | Documentation:
 |       https://github.com/davidB/kubectl-view-allocations
/
WARNING: You installed plugin "view-allocations" from the krew-index plugin repository.
    These plugins are not audited for security by the Krew maintainers.
    Run them at your own risk.
```

Figure 7.3 – Installing plugins using Krew

As you can see, installing `kubectl` plugins is so easy.

Using plugins

So, we have installed a few very useful plugins. Let's check out how to use them.

We have installed three plugins:

- `kubectl ctx`: This plugin allows us to easily to switch between Kubernetes clusters, which is very useful when you have more than one cluster set in your `kubeconfig`.

  Lets' check for available cluster by running the $ `kubectl ctx` command:

  ```
  gke_rimusz-lab1_us-central1-c_kubectl-lab
  docker-for-desktop
  docker-desktop
  3/3
  ```

  Figure 7.4 – The ctx plugin

- `kubectl ns`: This plugin allows us to switch between namespaces. Let's check for available namespaces in the cluster by running the $ `kubectl ns` command:

  ```
  test
  kube-system
  kube-public
  kube-node-lease
  default
  5/5
  ```

  Figure 7.5 – The ns plugin

- `kubectl view-allocations`: This plugin lists resource allocations of a namespace, such as CPU, memory, storage, and so on.

  Let's check for resources allocations in the cluster by running the $ `kubectl view-allocations` command:

```
 ~ $ kubectl view-allocations
Resource                                                    Requested  %Requested    Limit  %Limit  Allocatable     Free
attachable-volumes-gce-pd                                        0.0          0%      0.0      0%        127.0    127.0
  └ gke-kubectl-lab-default-pool-b3c7050d-5kff                   0.0          0%      0.0      0%        127.0    127.0
cpu                                                            638.0m        68%    201.0m     21%       940.0m   302.0m
  └ gke-kubectl-lab-default-pool-b3c7050d-5kff                 638.0m        68%    201.0m     21%       940.0m   302.0m
    ├ fluentbit-gke-tsqmf                                      100.0m                  0.0
    ├ gke-metrics-agent-l5cwb                                    2.0m                  0.0
    ├ kube-dns-54478649f-65xgs                                 260.0m                  0.0
    ├ kube-dns-autoscaler-645f7d66cf-nznqt                      20.0m                  0.0
    ├ kube-proxy-gke-kubectl-lab-default-pool-b3c7050d-5kff    100.0m                  0.0
    ├ l7-default-backend-678889f899-xcjf8                       10.0m                 10.0m
    ├ metrics-server-v0.3.6-5c699768b5-x6j7s                    48.0m                143.0m
    └ stackdriver-metadata-agent-cluster-level-9d79566c5-zx4ph  98.0m                 48.0m
ephemeral-storage                                                0.0          0%      0.0      0%         47.1G    47.1G
  └ gke-kubectl-lab-default-pool-b3c7050d-5kff                   0.0          0%      0.0      0%         47.1G    47.1G
memory                                                         667.0Mi       25%   1337.0Mi    51%         2.6Gi    1.3Gi
  └ gke-kubectl-lab-default-pool-b3c7050d-5kff                 667.0Mi       25%   1337.0Mi    51%         2.6Gi    1.3Gi
    ├ fluentbit-gke-tsqmf                                      200.0Mi               500.0Mi
    ├ gke-metrics-agent-l5cwb                                   20.0Mi                50.0Mi
    ├ kube-dns-54478649f-65xgs                                 110.0Mi               210.0Mi
    ├ kube-dns-autoscaler-645f7d66cf-nznqt                      10.0Mi                 0.0
    ├ l7-default-backend-678889f899-xcjf8                       20.0Mi                20.0Mi
    ├ metrics-server-v0.3.6-5c699768b5-x6j7s                   105.0Mi               355.0Mi
    └ stackdriver-metadata-agent-cluster-level-9d79566c5-zx4ph 202.0Mi               202.0Mi
pods                                                             0.0          0%      0.0      0%         55.0     55.0
  └ gke-kubectl-lab-default-pool-b3c7050d-5kff                   0.0          0%      0.0      0%         55.0     55.0
```

Figure 7.6 – The view-allocations plugin

You can see in the preceding list that using plugins looks as though these sub-commands are a part of kubectl tool itself.

Creating a basic plugin

In this section, let's create a simple plugin called toppods to show Kubernetes cluster nodes. It is just a very simple example of how to create the plugin:

1. We are going to create a simple bash-based plugin named kubectl-toppods:

    ```
    $ cat kubectl-toppods
    #!/bin/bash

    kubectl top pods
    ```

2. Let's copy the kubectl-toppods file to the ~/bin path:

    ```
    $ cp kubectl-toppods ~/bin
    ```

3. Make sure it is executable:

```
$ chmod +x ~/bin/ kubectl-toppods
```

4. Now let's try to run it:

```
$ kubectl toppods
NAME                             CPU(cores)    MEMORY(bytes)
postgresql-57578b68d9-6rpt8 1m                 22Mi
```

Nice! You can see that the plugin is working, and it is not very difficult to create a kubectl plugin.

Summary

In this chapter, we have learned how to install, use, and create kubectl plugins. It is useful to know how to expand kubectl with existing plugins, and how to create your ones.

We have learned about a few very handy and useful kubectl plugins:

- ctx: Allows us to switch between Kubernetes clusters very easily

- ns: Allows us to switch between namespaces

- view-allocations: Shows a list of allocations for resources in the cluster

When you work daily with multiple Kubernetes clusters and namespaces, using the ctx and ns plugins will save a lot of time.

In the next chapter, we going to learn how to deploy applications using Kustomize.

8
Introducing Kustomize for Kubernetes

In the previous chapter, we learned how to install, use, and create `kubectl` plugins.

In this chapter, let's learn how to use Kustomize for Kubernetes. Kustomize allows us to patch Kubernetes templates without changing the application's original templates. We are going to learn about Kustomize and how to patch Kubernetes deployments with its help.

In this chapter, we're going to cover the following main topics:

- Introduction to Kustomize
- Patching Kubernetes deployment

Introduction to Kustomize

Kustomize uses overlays for Kubernetes manifests to add, remove, or update configuration options without forking. What Kustomize does is take a Kubernetes template, patch it with specified changes in `kustomization.yaml`, and then deploy it to Kubernetes.

It is a handy tool for patching non-complex applications, for example, with changes needed for different environments or resource namespacing.

Kustomize is available as a standalone binary and as a native command in `kubectl` since v.1.14.

Let's look at a couple of Kustomize commands, use the following command:

- To show the generated modified templates on the terminal, use the following command:

```
$ kubectl kustomize base
```

- To deploy generated modified templates on Kubernetes:

```
$ kubectl apply -k base
```

In the preceding examples, `base` is the folder that has the application files and `kustomization.yaml`.

> **Note**
>
> The preceding commands will fail as there is no `base` folder. This is just an example of the commands.

Patching a Kubernetes application

In this section, let's try to patch an application with Kustomize. For this example, we have a `kustomize` folder with the following files:

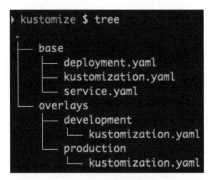

Figure 8.1 – Kustomize examples

The base folder has three files—deployment.yaml, service.yaml, and kustomization.yaml.

Let's check the deployment.yaml file by running the $ cat base/deployment.yaml command:

```
kustomize $ cat base/deployment.yaml
apiVersion: apps/v1
kind: Deployment
metadata:
  name: nginx
  labels:
    app: nginx
spec:
  replicas: 1
  selector:
    matchLabels:
      app: nginx
  template:
    metadata:
      labels:
        app: nginx
    spec:
      affinity:
        podAntiAffinity:
          requiredDuringSchedulingIgnoredDuringExecution:
          - labelSelector:
              matchExpressions:
              - key: app
                operator: In
                values:
                - nginx
            topologyKey: "kubernetes.io/hostname"
      containers:
      - image: nginx:1.18.0
        imagePullPolicy: IfNotPresent
        name: nginx
```

Figure 8.2 – The deployment.yaml file

In the preceding screenshot, we have the `nginx` deployment template, which we are going to use with Kustomize.

Let's get the `service.yaml` file's content by running the `$ cat base/service.yaml` command:

```
kustomize $ cat base/service.yaml
apiVersion: v1
kind: Service
metadata:
  name: nginx
  labels:
    app: nginx
spec:
  type: ClusterIP
  ports:
  - port: 80
    protocol: TCP
    targetPort: 80
  selector:
    app: nginx
```

Figure 8.3 – The service.yaml file

In the preceding screenshot, we have the `nginx` service template that we are going to use with Kustomize.

As you can see, we are using the `nginx` deployment and service template again so it will be easier for you to understand what Kustomize does.

Let's get the `kustomization.yaml.yaml` file's content by running the `$ cat base/kustomization.yaml` command:

```
> kustomize $ cat base/kustomization.yaml
apiVersion: kustomize.config.k8s.io/v1beta1
kind: Kustomization

images:
- name: nginx
  newTag: 1.19.1

resources:
- deployment.yaml
- service.yaml
```

Figure 8.4 – The kustomization.yaml file

As we are already familiar with the nginx deployment and service, let's take a look into the kustomization.yaml file.

With the following code from kustomization.yaml, we set a new tag for the nginx image:

```
```
images:
- name: nginx
  newTag: 1.19.1
```
```

The following code sets which resources to apply the settings to. As service does not have images, Kustomize will only apply to the deployment, but we will need service in the later steps, so we are setting it anyway:

```
```
resources:
- deployment.yaml
- service.yaml
```
```

Now, let's check how Kustomize will change the deployment by running the $kubectl kustomize base command:

```
) kustomize $ kubectl kustomize base
apiVersion: v1
kind: Service
metadata:
  labels:
    app: nginx
  name: nginx
spec:
  ports:
  - port: 80
    protocol: TCP
    targetPort: 80
  selector:
    app: nginx
  type: ClusterIP
---
apiVersion: apps/v1
kind: Deployment
metadata:
  labels:
    app: nginx
  name: nginx
spec:
  replicas: 1
  selector:
    matchLabels:
      app: nginx
  template:
    metadata:
      labels:
        app: nginx
    spec:
      affinity:
        podAntiAffinity:
          requiredDuringSchedulingIgnoredDuringExecution:
          - labelSelector:
              matchExpressions:
              - key: app
                operator: In
                values:
                - nginx
            topologyKey: kubernetes.io/hostname
      containers:
      - image: nginx:1.19.1
        imagePullPolicy: IfNotPresent
        name: nginx
```

Figure 8.5 – kubectl kustomize base output

From the preceding output, you can see that Kustomize generated service and deployment content. The contents of service did not change, but let's take a look at deployment. Comparing the original file, base/deployment.yaml, with the preceding output, we see that - image: nginx:1.18.0 got changed to - image: nginx:1.19.1, as was specified in the kustomization.yaml file.

It's a nice and easy `image` tag change without modifying the original `deployment.yaml` file.

> **Note**
>
> Such tricks come handy, especially in real-world application deployments, where different environments might use different Docker image tags.

Kustomize overlays

As a sysadmin, I want to be able to deploy different environments (development and production) of my web service with dedicated custom configurations, such as the number of replicas, allocated resources, security rules, or other configurations. I would like to do this without maintaining duplications of my core application configurations.

In this section, let's learn more advanced customizations using Kustomize to deploy to development and production environments and using different namespaces and NGINX Docker tags for each environment.

In the `overlays` folder, we have the `development/kustomization.yaml` and `production/kustomization.yaml` files; let's check them. In the following screenshot, we have the `kustomization.yaml` file, which will be applied to the development environment.

Let's get the `overlays/development/kustomization.yaml` file's content by running the `$ cat overlays/development/kustomization.yaml` command:

```
▶ kustomize $ cat overlays/development/kustomization.yaml
apiVersion: kustomize.config.k8s.io/v1beta1
kind: Kustomization

resources:
- ../../base

nameSuffix: -development

commonLabels:
  environment: development

namespace: nginx-dev
```

Figure 8.6 – The development/kustomization.yaml content

In the preceding screenshot, we have the `kustomization.yaml` file, which will be applied to the development environment.

Let's get the `overlays/production/kustomization.yaml` file's content by running the `$ cat overlays/development/kustomization.yaml` command:

```
▶ kustomize $ cat overlays/production/kustomization.yaml
apiVersion: kustomize.config.k8s.io/v1beta1
kind: Kustomization

resources:
- ../../base

nameSuffix: -production

commonLabels:
  environment: production

namespace: nginx-prod

images:
- name: nginx
  newTag: 1.19.2
```

Figure 8.7 – The production/kustomization.yaml content

In the preceding screenshot, we have the `kustomization.yaml` file, which will be applied to the production environment.

OK, let's check the changes we are getting in the `development/kustomization.yaml` file:

```
resources:
- ../../base # setting where the main templates are stored
nameSuffix: -development # updating service/deployment name
commonLabels:
  environment: development # add new label
namespace: nginx-dev # setting namespace
```

Let's see how these changes will be applied to the development `deployment` and `service` by running the $ `kubectl kustomize overlays/development` command:

```
▶ kustomize $ kubectl kustomize overlays/development
apiVersion: v1
kind: Service
metadata:
  labels:
    app: nginx
    environment: development
  name: nginx-development
  namespace: nginx-dev
spec:
  ports:
  - port: 80
    protocol: TCP
    targetPort: 80
  selector:
    app: nginx
    environment: development
  type: ClusterIP
---
apiVersion: apps/v1
kind: Deployment
metadata:
  labels:
    app: nginx
    environment: development
  name: nginx-development
  namespace: nginx-dev
spec:
  replicas: 1
  selector:
    matchLabels:
      app: nginx
      environment: development
  template:
    metadata:
      labels:
        app: nginx
        environment: development
    spec:
      affinity:
        podAntiAffinity:
          requiredDuringSchedulingIgnoredDuringExecution:
          - labelSelector:
              matchExpressions:
              - key: app
                operator: In
                values:
                - nginx
            topologyKey: kubernetes.io/hostname
      containers:
      - image: nginx:1.19.1
        imagePullPolicy: IfNotPresent
        name: nginx
```

Figure 8.8 – The kubectl kustomize overlays/development output

As we can see, the deployment and service names were changed, a namespace was added, and the nginx image tag was changed as per the kustomization.yaml file in the base folder specification. Great job so far!

Now let's check the production/kustomization.yaml file:

```
resources:
- ../../base # setting where the main templates are stored
nameSuffix: -production # updating service/deployment name
commonLabels:
  environment: production # add new label
namespace: nginx-prod # setting namespace
images:
- name: nginx
  newTag: 1.19.2 # tag gets changed
```

The changes we want to apply are very similar to the ones made for development, but we also want a different Docker image tag to be set.

Let's see how it is going to work out by running the $ kubectl kustomize overlays/production command:

```
> kustomize $ kubectl kustomize overlays/production
apiVersion: v1
kind: Service
metadata:
  labels:
    app: nginx
    environment: production
  name: nginx-production
  namespace: nginx-prod
spec:
  ports:
  - port: 80
    protocol: TCP
    targetPort: 80
  selector:
    app: nginx
    environment: production
  type: ClusterIP
---
apiVersion: apps/v1
kind: Deployment
metadata:
  labels:
    app: nginx
    environment: production
  name: nginx-production
  namespace: nginx-prod
spec:
  replicas: 1
  selector:
    matchLabels:
      app: nginx
      environment: production
  template:
    metadata:
      labels:
        app: nginx
        environment: production
    spec:
      affinity:
        podAntiAffinity:
          requiredDuringSchedulingIgnoredDuringExecution:
          - labelSelector:
              matchExpressions:
              - key: app
                operator: In
                values:
                - nginx
            topologyKey: kubernetes.io/hostname
      containers:
      - image: nginx:1.19.2
        imagePullPolicy: IfNotPresent
        name: nginx
```

Figure 8.9 – The kubectl kustomize overlays/production output

As you can see, all the required changes were applied.

> **Note**
>
> Kustomize merges all found `kustomization.yaml` files, and files from the `base` folder get applied first, then the files from the `overlay` folder. You can choose how to name your folders.

Now, it is time to actually perform an installation using Kustomize:

```
$ kubectl create ns nginx-prod
namespace/nginx-prod created
$ kubectl apply -k overlays/production/
service/nginx-prod created
deployment.apps/nginx-production created
$ kubectl get pods -n nginx-prod
NAME                          READY   STATUS     RESTARTS   AGE
nginx-production-dc9cbdb6-j4ws4   1/1     Running    0
17s
```

With the preceding commands, we have created the `nginx-prod` namespace and installed the `nginx` application with the help of the Kustomize-applied changes, which you can see it running.

We have learned only some basic functionalities of Kustomize, as it is out of scope to cover everything about Kustomize in this book, so please refer to the following link for more information: `https://kustomize.io/`.

Summary

In this chapter, we have learned how to install applications using Kustomize.

We have learned how to apply Kustomize to `nginx` deployments and services, changing their names, adding namespace, and changing the image tag in the deployment. All that was done without changing the application's original templates by using `kustomization.yaml` files with Kustomize to make the required changes.

In the next chapter, we are going to learn how to use Helm—the Kubernetes package manager.

9
Introducing Helm for Kubernetes

In the previous chapter, we learned how to install and use Kustomize. In this chapter, let's learn about Helm (`https://helm.sh`).

Helm is the de facto Kubernetes package manager, and one of the best and easiest ways to install any kind of complex application on Kubernetes.

Helm is not part of `kubectl`, nor does it have a `kubectl` plugin, but it plays a big role in the Kubernetes space and is a must-know tool.

In this chapter, we are going to learn about Helm v3, in particular, how to install applications, upgrade and roll back application releases, create and lint Helm charts, and extend Helm with plugins.

> **Note**
> We are going to use Helm v3 as it was the latest version of Helm at the time of writing.

We're going to cover the following main topics in this chapter:

- Introduction to Helm

- Installing applications using Helm charts

- Upgrading Helm releases

- Rolling back to a previous Helm release

- Using Helm's template command

- Creating a Helm chart

- Using Helm's linting feature

- Extending Helm with plugins

Introduction to Helm

Helm is a Kubernetes package manager that allows developers and users an easy way to package, configure, share, and deploy Kubernetes applications onto Kubernetes clusters.

You can think of Helm as the same as the Homebrew/APT/Yum package managers, but for Kubernetes.

Helm v3 is based on a client-only architecture. It connects to the Kubernetes API the same way as `kubectl` does, by using a `kubeconfig` file containing the Kubernetes cluster connection settings. So where `kubectl` works, the Helm CLI will work too, using the same `kubectl` capabilities and permissions.

To better understand Helm, you should get familiar with the following concepts:

- **The Helm CLI**: A command-line tool that interacts with the Kubernetes API and does various functions, such as installing, upgrading, and deleting Helm releases.

- **A chart**: This is a collection of template files that describe Kubernetes resources.

- **Chart templating**: Helm chart templating language used in the charts.

- **A repository**: A Helm repository is a location where packaged charts are stored and shared.

- **A release**: A specific instance of a chart deployed to a Kubernetes cluster.

Let's take a look at each one of them in detail in the following sections.

The Helm CLI

The Helm CLI can be installed on different operating systems using the following commands:

- Installing on macOS is done as follows:

```
$ brew install helm
```

- Installing on Windows is done with the following command:

```
$ choco install kubernetes-helm
```

- Installing on Linux is done as follows:

```
$ https://raw.githubusercontent.com/helm/helm/master/
scripts/get-helm-3 | bash
```

You can get all available Helm CLI commands with `helm -h`. Let's list the most used ones, along with their descriptions:

- `helm repo add`: Adds a Helm chart repository to the local cache list, after which we can reference it to pull charts from the repository.

- `helm repo update`: Gets the latest information about chart repositories; the information is stored locally.

- `helm search repo`: Searches for charts in the given repositories.

- `helm pull`: Downloads a given chart from the chart repository.

- `helm upgrade -i`: If there is no release then install it, otherwise upgrade the release.

- `helm ls`: Lists releases in the current namespace. If the `-A` flag is provided, it will list all the namespaces.

- `helm history`: Prints historical revisions for a given release.

- `helm rollback`: Rolls back a release to a previous revision.

- `helm template`: Renders chart templates locally and displays the output.

- `helm create`: Creates a chart.

- `helm lint`: Lints a chart.

- `helm plugin`: Installs, lists, updates, and uninstalls Helm plugins.

Let's learn each one of these in more detail in the following sections.

Helm charts

A chart is a Helm package. It is a collection of template files that describe Kubernetes resources. It uses templating to create Kubernetes manifests.

An example Helm chart structure is shown as follows:

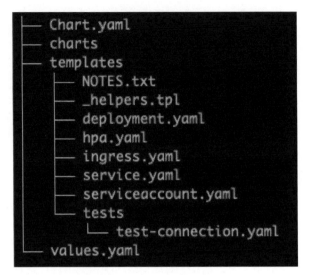

```
├── Chart.yaml
├── charts
├── templates
│   ├── NOTES.txt
│   ├── _helpers.tpl
│   ├── deployment.yaml
│   ├── hpa.yaml
│   ├── ingress.yaml
│   ├── service.yaml
│   ├── serviceaccount.yaml
│   └── tests
│       └── test-connection.yaml
└── values.yaml
```

Figure 9.1 – Chart folders layout

Let's discuss some of the preceding contents in detail:

- `Chart.yaml`: The file that contains information about the chart's metadata.
- `charts`: The folder where sub-charts get stored.
- `templates`: The folder where template files get stored.
- `values.yaml`: A YAML-formatted file with configuration values used by the chart templates. These values can be resources, replica counts, or an image repository and tag, among other things.

> **Tip**
> To change values, it is recommended to use the `override-values.yaml` file, in which you just enter the values you want to change. Changing the default `values.yaml` file that comes with the chart is not recommended, as you might lose track of changes in the newer versions of the file.

Now that we have learned some of the basics of the Helm chart structure, let's dive into chart templating.

Chart templating

The strongest feature of Helm is chart templating. The Helm template language is based on the Go language package `text/template` syntax. Values used with templating syntax can be employed to customize Kubernetes resource manifests. Before chart installation, Helm renders the chart's templates by injecting specified values and then does the chart install.

Values are read from the default `values.yaml` file that comes with the chart, or a user-provided file, for example, named `override-values.yaml`. Both files' values will be combined and then applied to the chart.

Let's take a look at the following chart template example:

```
apiVersion: v1
kind: Service
metadata:
  name: {{ include "nginx.fullname" . }}
  labels:
    {{- include "nginx.labels" . | nindent 4 }}
spec:
  type: {{ .Values.service.type }}
  ports:
    - port: {{ .Values.service.port }}
      targetPort: http
      protocol: TCP
      name: http
  selector:
    {{- include "nginx.selectorLabels" . | nindent 4 }}
```

Figure 9.2 – Chart template example

The preceding code snippet of the Helm template, which is a Kubernetes service resource, allows us to set the service type and port. If the default values do not suit your requirements, you can change the default values by providing new ones using a custom `override-values.yaml` file.

Other values such as name, labels, and selector get injected from the _helpers.
tpl file, which is the default location for template partials:

```
{{/*
Common labels
*/}}
{{- define "nginx.labels" -}}
helm.sh/chart: {{ include "nginx.chart" . }}
{{ include "nginx.selectorLabels" . }}
{{- if .Chart.AppVersion }}
app.kubernetes.io/version: {{ .Chart.AppVersion | quote }}
{{- end }}
app.kubernetes.io/managed-by: {{ .Release.Service }}
{{- end }}

{{/*
Selector labels
*/}}
{{- define "nginx.selectorLabels" -}}
app.kubernetes.io/name: {{ include "nginx.name" . }}
app.kubernetes.io/instance: {{ .Release.Name }}
{{- end }}
```

Figure 9.3 – A partial example of _helpers.tpl

The preceding code snippet is of a _helpers.tpl file that defines labels and the selector
to be injected into the chart's templates.

Repositories

A repository is a location where packaged charts are stored and shared. It can be any web
server capable of serving files. Charts in a repository are stored in the compressed .tgz
format.

Releases

A release is a specific instance of a chart deployed to a Kubernetes cluster. One Helm chart
can be installed many times using the same release name, and each time a new release
version will be created.

The release information for a particular release is stored in the same namespace as the
release itself.

You can install the same Helm chart using the same release name but a different
namespace an infinite number of times.

Now that we have learned some of the basics of Helm, let's dive into installing applications using charts.

Installing applications using Helm charts

There are many Helm chart repositories, and it is way too much hassle to set them all up one by one.

Instead, we are going to use as our central Helm chart repository `https://chartcenter.io`, which has over 300 Helm repositories and can be our single source of truth to install all the charts from one location. It also has a nice UI where you can search for charts and get very informative details about them:

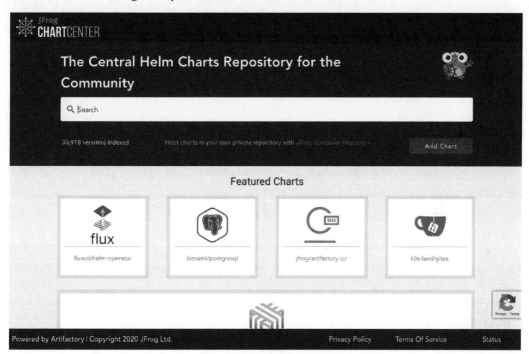

Figure 9.4 – ChartCenter UI

The preceding screenshot shows the ChartCenter **UI**.

It is also very easy to set ChartCenter as your central Helm repository, as follows:

```
$ helm repo add center https://repo.chartcenter.io
"center" has been added to your repositories
$ helm repo update
Hang tight while we grab the latest from your chart
```

```
repositories...

...Successfully got an update from the "center" chart
repository

Update Complete. Happy Helming!
```

The preceding commands added the center chart repository and updated the Helm local cache with its content.

Now we can try searching for the postgresql chart by running the $ helm search repo center/bitnami/postgresql -l | head -n 5 command:

```
charts $ helm search repo center/bitnami/postgresql -l | head -n 5
NAME                         CHART VERSION   APP VERSION   DESCRIPTION
center/bitnami/postgresql    9.3.2           11.9.0        Chart for PostgreSQL, an object-relational data...
center/bitnami/postgresql    9.2.1           11.9.0        Chart for PostgreSQL, an object-relational data...
center/bitnami/postgresql    9.2.0           11.8.0        Chart for PostgreSQL, an object-relational data...
center/bitnami/postgresql    9.1.4           11.8.0        Chart for PostgreSQL, an object-relational data...
```

Figure 9.5 – Searching for the PostgreSQL chart

In the preceding screenshot, we can see that we got the latest five versions of the Bitnami PostgreSQL chart.

Before installing the PostgreSQL chart, we should set a password, as it is a good practice to set your own password instead of using one generated by Helm charts.

By reading the chart's README at https://chartcenter.io/bitnami/ postgresql, we can find the value name we need to use:

postgresqlPostgresPassword	PostgreSQL admin password (used when postgresqlUsername is not postgres , in which case postgres is the admin username).	*random 10 character alphanumeric string*
postgresqlUsername	PostgreSQL user (creates a non-admin user when postgresqlUsername is not postgres)	postgres
postgresqlPassword	PostgreSQL user password	*random 10 character alphanumeric string*
postgresqlDatabase	PostgreSQL database	nil

Figure 9.6 – PostgreSQL chart password

The preceding screenshot shows us that the postgresqlPassword variable in the values.yaml file is needed to set the password for the PostgreSQL chart.

First, let's create a password-values.yaml file to store the PostgreSQL password:

```
$ echo "postgresqlPassword: SomeVerySecurePassword" > password-
values.yaml
```

And let's install it using the following command:

```
$ helm upgrade -i postgresql center/bitnami/postgresql
--version=9.2.1 -f password-values.yaml
```

The output for the preceding command is shown in the following screenshot:

```
> charts $ helm upgrade -i postgresql center/bitnami/postgresql --version=9.2.1 -f password-values.yaml
Release "postgresql" does not exist. Installing it now.
NAME: postgresql
LAST DEPLOYED: Thu Aug 20 20:20:43 2020
NAMESPACE: default
STATUS: deployed
REVISION: 1
TEST SUITE: None
NOTES:
** Please be patient while the chart is being deployed **

PostgreSQL can be accessed via port 5432 on the following DNS name from within your cluster:

    postgresql.default.svc.cluster.local - Read/Write connection

To get the password for "postgres" run:

    export POSTGRES_PASSWORD=$(kubectl get secret --namespace default postgresql -o jsonpath="{.data.postgresql-password}" | base64 --decode)

To connect to your database run the following command:

    kubectl run postgresql-client --rm --tty -i --restart='Never' --namespace default --image docker.io/bitnami/postgresql:11.9.0-debian-10-r
0 --env="PGPASSWORD=$POSTGRES_PASSWORD" --command -- psql --host postgresql -U postgres -d postgres -p 5432

To connect to your database from outside the cluster execute the following commands:

    kubectl port-forward --namespace default svc/postgresql 5432:5432 &
    PGPASSWORD="$POSTGRES_PASSWORD" psql --host 127.0.0.1 -U postgres -d postgres -p 5432
```

Figure 9.7 – Helm installing the PostgreSQL chart

The preceding command installed the PostgreSQL chart with the name `postgresql` into the current namespace.

> **Tip**
> The preceding `helm upgrade` command has an `-i` flag (with the long name of `--install`), which allows us to use the same command for both the first install and the following upgrades afterward.

Let's check what was installed with the chart using the following command:

```
$ kubectl get all
```

The output of the preceding command is shown in the following screenshot:

```
▶ charts $ kubectl get all
NAME                           READY   STATUS    RESTARTS   AGE
pod/postgresql-postgresql-0    1/1     Running   0          111s

NAME                          TYPE        CLUSTER-IP    EXTERNAL-IP   PORT(S)    AGE
service/kubernetes            ClusterIP   10.16.0.1     <none>        443/TCP    75d
service/postgresql            ClusterIP   10.16.15.71   <none>        5432/TCP   111s
service/postgresql-headless   ClusterIP   None          <none>        5432/TCP   111s

NAME                                     READY   AGE
statefulset.apps/postgresql-postgresql   1/1     112s
```

Figure 9.8 – Listing all installed resources

In the preceding screenshot, we can see the postgresql pod, two postgresql-related services, and statefulset. Looking at service/postgresql, we can see that postgresql can be accessed by other Kubernetes applications on postgresql:5432.

Let's check that all secrets were properly created by running the following command:

```
$ kubectl get secret
```

The output of the preceding command is shown in the following screenshot:

```
▶ charts $ kubectl get secret
NAME                              TYPE                                   DATA   AGE
default-token-44sr7               kubernetes.io/service-account-token    3      75d
postgresql                        Opaque                                 1      15m
sh.helm.release.v1.postgresql.v1  helm.sh/release.v1                     1      15m
```

Figure 9.9 – Listing all installed secrets

In the preceding screenshot, we see the postgresql secret where the PostgreSQL password is stored, and sh.helm.release.v1.postgresql.v1, where the Helm release information is stored.

Now, let's check for Helm releases in the current namespace by running the following command:

```
$ helm ls
```

The output of the preceding command is shown in the following screenshot:

Figure 9.10 – Listing Helm releases

In the preceding screenshot, we see a successfully deployed Helm release of `postgresql`, where we have a list of the following:

- `STATUS`: Shows the release status as `deployed`

- `CHART`: Shows the chart name and version as `postgresql-9.2.1`

- `APP VERSION`: Shows the PostgreSQL version; in this case, `11.9.0`

This was easy to install – we just had to provide the password, and boom, we have a fully installed PostgreSQL instance, and its password is even stored in the secret.

Upgrading Helm releases

In the previous section, we installed PostgreSQL, so now let's try and upgrade it. We need to know how to do this because it will have to be upgraded from time to time.

For the upgrade, we are going to use the latest available PostgreSQL chart version, that is, `9.3.2`.

Let's get and run the upgrade with the following command:

```
$ helm upgrade -i postgresql center/bitnami/postgresql
--version=9.3.2 -f password-values.yaml
```

The output of the preceding command is shown in the following screenshot:

```
 charts $ helm upgrade -i postgresql center/bitnami/postgresql --version=9.3.2 -f password-values.yaml
Release "postgresql" has been upgraded. Happy Helming!
NAME: postgresql
LAST DEPLOYED: Thu Aug 20 20:58:45 2020
NAMESPACE: default
STATUS: deployed
REVISION: 2
TEST SUITE: None
NOTES:
** Please be patient while the chart is being deployed **

PostgreSQL can be accessed via port 5432 on the following DNS name from within your cluster:

    postgresql.default.svc.cluster.local - Read/Write connection

To get the password for "postgres" run:

    export POSTGRES_PASSWORD=$(kubectl get secret --namespace default postgresql -o jsonpath="{.data.postgresql-password}" | base64 --decode)

To connect to your database run the following command:

    kubectl run postgresql-client --rm --tty -i --restart='Never' --namespace default --image docker.io/bitnami/postgresql:11.9.0-debian-10-r
1 --env="PGPASSWORD=$POSTGRES_PASSWORD" --command -- psql --host postgresql -U postgres -d postgres -p 5432


To connect to your database from outside the cluster execute the following commands:

    kubectl port-forward --namespace default svc/postgresql 5432:5432 &
    PGPASSWORD="$POSTGRES_PASSWORD" psql --host 127.0.0.1 -U postgres -d postgres -p 5432
 charts $ kubectl get all
NAME                          READY   STATUS    RESTARTS   AGE
pod/postgresql-postgresql-0   0/1     Running   0          18s

NAME                         TYPE        CLUSTER-IP     EXTERNAL-IP   PORT(S)    AGE
service/kubernetes           ClusterIP   10.16.0.1      <none>        443/TCP    75d
service/postgresql           ClusterIP   10.16.15.71    <none>        5432/TCP   38m
service/postgresql-headless  ClusterIP   None           <none>        5432/TCP   38m

NAME                                    READY   AGE
statefulset.apps/postgresql-postgresql  0/1     38m
 charts $ helm ls
NAME        NAMESPACE   REVISION   UPDATED                             STATUS     CHART             APP VERSION
postgresql  default     2          2020-08-20 20:58:45.326837 +0300 EEST   deployed   postgresql-9.3.2  11.9.0
```

Figure 9.11 – Listing Helm releases

We ran the preceding `helm upgrade` command to change the `postgresql` chart version to `9.3.2`, but we see the PostgreSQL version is still the same as it was, that is, `11.9.0`, so that means the chart itself received some changes, but the application version was kept the same.

Running `helm ls` shows `REVISION 2`, which means the second release for the PostgreSQL chart.

Let's check the secrets one more time by running the following command:

```
$ kubectl get secrets
```

The output of the preceding command is shown in the following screenshot:

```
> charts $ kubectl get secrets
NAME                                TYPE                                    DATA    AGE
default-token-44sr7                 kubernetes.io/service-account-token     3       75d
postgresql                          Opaque                                  1       48m
sh.helm.release.v1.postgresql.v1    helm.sh/release.v1                      1       48m
sh.helm.release.v1.postgresql.v2    helm.sh/release.v1                      1       10m
```

Figure 9.12 – Listing Helm releases

From the preceding screenshot, we can see a new secret, `sh.helm.release.v1.postgresql.v2`, which is where the PostgreSQL upgrade release was stored.

It's nice to see how Helm keeps track of all releases and allows easy application upgrades with a single `helm upgrade` command.

> **Note**
>
> A Helm release contains all Kubernetes templates from the chart, which make it much easier to track them (from the perspective of releases) as one single unit.

Let's learn how to do a release rollback. We'll do this because, from time to time, releases can go bad and need to be rolled back.

Rolling back to a previous Helm release

In this section, let's see how to roll back to a previous version using the `helm rollback` command.

The `helm rollback` command is unique to Helm, and it allows us to roll back the whole application, so you do not have to worry about which Kubernetes resources need to be rolled back specifically.

Of course, when dealing with the release IDs of real-world applications, database schemas get changed as well, so to roll back the frontend application, you have to roll back the database schema changes too. This means that things aren't always so straightforward as they may seem here, but using Helm still simplifies some parts of the application release rollback process.

To run the `helm rollback` command, we first need to know the release revision we want to roll back to, which we can find with the following command:

```
$ helm history postgresql
```

The output of the preceding command is shown in the following screenshot:

```
charts $ helm history postgresql
REVISION     UPDATED                STATUS       CHART            APP VERSION   DESCRIPTION
1            Thu Aug 20 20:20:43 2020   superseded   postgresql-9.2.1   11.9.0        Install complete
2            Thu Aug 20 20:58:45 2020   deployed     postgresql-9.3.2   11.9.0        Upgrade complete
```

Figure 9.13 – Listing Helm release revisions

In the preceding `helm history postgresql` command, we got a list of release revisions.

So, we want to roll back `postgresql` to revision `1`:

```
$ helm rollback postgresql 1
```

The output of the preceding command is shown in the following screenshot:

```
charts $ helm rollback postgresql 1
Rollback was a success! Happy Helming!
charts $ kubectl get all
NAME                          READY   STATUS             RESTARTS   AGE
pod/postgresql-postgresql-0   0/1     ContainerCreating  0          4s

NAME                          TYPE        CLUSTER-IP     EXTERNAL-IP   PORT(S)    AGE
service/kubernetes            ClusterIP   10.16.0.1      <none>        443/TCP    75d
service/postgresql            ClusterIP   10.16.15.71    <none>        5432/TCP   62m
service/postgresql-headless   ClusterIP   None           <none>        5432/TCP   62m

NAME                                    READY   AGE
statefulset.apps/postgresql-postgresql  0/1     62m
charts $ helm ls
NAME         NAMESPACE   REVISION   UPDATED                          STATUS     CHART              APP VERSION
postgresql   default     3          2020-08-20 21:22:48.13673 +0300 EEST   deployed   postgresql-9.2.1   11.9.0
charts $ helm history postgresql
REVISION     UPDATED                STATUS       CHART            APP VERSION   DESCRIPTION
1            Thu Aug 20 20:20:43 2020   superseded   postgresql-9.2.1   11.9.0        Install complete
2            Thu Aug 20 20:58:45 2020   superseded   postgresql-9.3.2   11.9.0        Upgrade complete
3            Thu Aug 20 21:22:48 2020   deployed     postgresql-9.2.1   11.9.0        Rollback to 1
```

Figure 9.14 – Helm rollback release

In the preceding screenshot, we see that the rollback was done with the `helm rollback postgresql 1` command and now we see three revisions, as even when doing a rollback, a new release gets created.

As you can see, rolling back to the previous release is quite easy.

Using Helm's template command

With Helm's `helm template` command, you can check the output of the chart in fully rendered Kubernetes resource templates. This is a very handy command to check the templates' outputs, especially when you are developing a new chart, making changes to the chart, debugging, and so on.

So, let's check it out by running the following command:

```
$ helm template postgresql center/bitnami/postgresql
--version=9.3.2 -f password-values.yaml
```

The preceding command will print all templates on the screen. Of course, you can pipe it out to the file as well.

As the output is very long, we aren't going to print all of it, but only parts of the Kubernetes manifest:

```
---
# Source: postgresql/templates/secrets.yaml
apiVersion: v1
kind: Secret
metadata:
  name: postgresql
...
---
# Source: postgresql/templates/svc-headless.yaml
apiVersion: v1
kind: Service
metadata:
  name: postgresql-headless
...
---
# Source: postgresql/templates/svc.yaml
apiVersion: v1
kind: Service
metadata:
  name: postgresql
...
---
# Source: postgresql/templates/statefulset.yaml
apiVersion: apps/v1
kind: StatefulSet
metadata:
  name: postgresql-postgresql
...
```

The preceding output shows all of the resources that are part of the `postgresql` chart. The resources are divided with `---`.

`helm template` is a powerful command for checking a chart's templates and printing the output so you read it through. `helm template` doesn't connect to the Kubernetes cluster, it only fills the templates with values and prints the output.

You can achieve the same thing by adding `--dry-run --debug` flags to the `helm upgrade` command. With this, Helm will validate the templates against the Kubernetes cluster.

An example of the full command would look as follows:

```
$ helm template postgresql center/bitnami/postgresql
--version=9.3.2 -f password-values.yaml --dry-run --debug
```

We have learned a few handy Helm commands to be used before installing or upgrading our Helm release.

Another strong use case for using `helm template` is to render templates to a file and then compare them. This is useful for comparing chart versions or the impact of customized parameters on the final output.

Creating a Helm chart

We have learned many cool tricks we can do with Helm! Let's now learn how to create a Helm chart.

The `helm create` command creates an example chart for you, so you can use it as a base and update it with the required Kubernetes resources, values, and so on. It creates a fully working `nginx` chart, so we are going to name the chart by that name.

Let's now check how easy it is to create a chart by running the following command:

```
$ helm create nginx
```

The output of the preceding command is shown in the following screenshot:

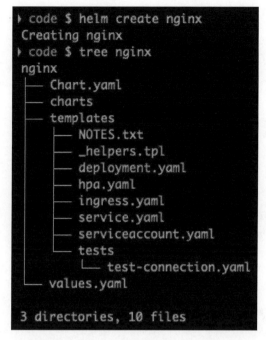

```
▸ code $ helm create nginx
Creating nginx
▸ code $ tree nginx
nginx
├── Chart.yaml
├── charts
├── templates
│   ├── NOTES.txt
│   ├── _helpers.tpl
│   ├── deployment.yaml
│   ├── hpa.yaml
│   ├── ingress.yaml
│   ├── service.yaml
│   ├── serviceaccount.yaml
│   └── tests
│       └── test-connection.yaml
└── values.yaml

3 directories, 10 files
```

Figure 9.15 – The helm create command

In the preceding screenshot, we ran the `helm create nginx` command, where `nginx` is our chart name. The name is also used to create a new folder where the chart content will be stored. The folder structure is shown using the `tree nginx` command.

As you can see in the screenshot, the `deployment.yaml` file, **Horizontal Pod Autoscaler (HPA)**, `ingress`, `service`, and `serviceaccount` resource templates have been created, all of which provide a good base to start from.

The preceding command also created the `test-connection.yaml` file so we can run a test with `helm test` against the installed `nginx` chart.

Now let's install the chart by running the following command:

```
$ helm install nginx nginx
```

The output of the preceding command is shown in the following screenshot:

```
▶ code $ helm install nginx nginx
NAME: nginx
LAST DEPLOYED: Fri Sep  4 19:48:50 2020
NAMESPACE: default
STATUS: deployed
REVISION: 1
NOTES:
1. Get the application URL by running these commands:
   export POD_NAME=$(kubectl get pods --namespace default -l "app.kubernetes.io/name=nginx
,app.kubernetes.io/instance=nginx" -o jsonpath="{.items[0].metadata.name}")
   echo "Visit http://127.0.0.1:8080 to use your application"
   kubectl --namespace default port-forward $POD_NAME 8080:80
▶ code $ kubectl get all -l "app.kubernetes.io/name=nginx"
NAME                          READY    STATUS     RESTARTS    AGE
pod/nginx-fcb5d6b64-b5cl9     1/1      Running    0           6m35s

NAME               TYPE        CLUSTER-IP      EXTERNAL-IP    PORT(S)    AGE
service/nginx      ClusterIP   10.16.6.108     <none>         80/TCP     6m35s

NAME                        READY    UP-TO-DATE    AVAILABLE    AGE
deployment.apps/nginx       1/1      1             1            6m36s

NAME                                  DESIRED    CURRENT    READY    AGE
replicaset.apps/nginx-fcb5d6b64       1          1          1        6m36s
```

Figure 9.16 – Installing the nginx chart

In the preceding screenshot, we ran `helm install nginx nginx`. This command uses the following basic syntax:

```
helm install <RELEASE NAME> <CHART NAME>
```

Here, `<CHART NAME>` is the local folder, so note that you can install the chart from remote Helm repositories and also from local folders, both with the same command.

The next command we used is as follows:

```
kubectl get all -l "app.kubernetes.io/name=nginx"
```

This command helped us to show the resources deployed by default by the chart.

As we already mentioned the `helm test` command, let's check out how that command functions:

```
$ helm test nginx
```

The output of the preceding command is shown in the following screenshot:

```
› code $ helm test nginx
Pod nginx-test-connection pending
Pod nginx-test-connection succeeded
NAME: nginx
LAST DEPLOYED: Fri Sep  4 19:48:50 2020
NAMESPACE: default
STATUS: deployed
REVISION: 1
TEST SUITE:    nginx-test-connection
Last Started:   Fri Sep  4 20:13:17 2020
Last Completed: Fri Sep  4 20:13:19 2020
Phase:          Succeeded
NOTES:
1. Get the application URL by running these commands:
   export POD_NAME=$(kubectl get pods --namespace default -l "app.kubernetes.io/name=nginx
,app.kubernetes.io/instance=nginx" -o jsonpath="{.items[0].metadata.name}")
   echo "Visit http://127.0.0.1:8080 to use your application"
   kubectl --namespace default port-forward $POD_NAME 8080:80
› code $
› code $ kubectl get pods
NAME                       READY    STATUS      RESTARTS    AGE
nginx-fcb5d6b64-b5cl9      1/1      Running     0           29m
nginx-test-connection      0/1      Completed   0           5m7s
```

Figure 9.17 – Testing the nginx chart

The preceding `helm test nginx` command runs the test against the Helm release named `nginx`. The output of the `kubectl get pods` command shows the `nginx-test-connection` pod that was used to run the chart test and was then stopped.

Next, let's check the contents of the `test-connection.yaml` file:

```
$ cat nginx/templates/tests/test-connection.yaml
```

The output of the preceding command is shown in the following screenshot:

```
› code $ cat nginx/templates/tests/test-connection.yaml
apiVersion: v1
kind: Pod
metadata:
  name: "{{ include "nginx.fullname" . }}-test-connection"
  labels:
    {{- include "nginx.labels" . | nindent 4 }}
  annotations:
    "helm.sh/hook": test-success
spec:
  containers:
    - name: wget
      image: busybox
      command: ['wget']
      args: ['{{ include "nginx.fullname" . }}:{{ .Values.service.port }}']
  restartPolicy: Never
```

Figure 9.18 – test-connection.yaml content

In the preceding screenshot, you can see a simple pod template that runs the `curl` command against the `nginx` service resource.

This `args: ['{{ include "nginx.fullname" . }}:{{ .Values. service.port }}']` line of template code gets converted to `nginx:80` when the actual Kubernetes resource gets created.

Simple and easy, right? As we can see, the `helm create` command creates a working chart with the example resource templates, and even with the test template.

Using Helm's linting feature

So far, we've learned how to create a Helm chart. However, we also need to know how to check the chart for possible issues and errors. For that, we can use the `helm lint <CHART NAME>` command, which will check the Helm chart content by running a series of tests to verify the chart integrity.

Let's `lint` the `nginx` chart we have created:

```
$ helm lint nginx
```

The output of the preceding command is shown in the following screenshot:

```
▸ code $ helm lint nginx
===> Linting nginx
[INFO] Chart.yaml: icon is recommended

1 chart(s) linted, 0 chart(s) failed
```

Figure 9.19 – Linting the nginx chart

As you can see in the preceding screenshot, our chart has no issues and can be installed safely. The `[INFO]` message is just the warning that the chart's icon is missing, which can be safely ignored.

It is really recommend to have it if you want to host your charts for example in `https://chartcenter.io` where it gets shown in its UI.

Extending Helm with plugins

Helm can be extended with plugins as well. Plugins are useful to extend Helm features that are not part of the Helm CLI, as Helm might not have everything that you need.

There is no central Helm plugins repository yet, where you would be able to see a list of all available plugins, nor is there a Helm plugin manager.

As most of the plugins are stored in GitHub repositories, and it is recommended to use the GitHub topic `helm-plugin` to label the plugin, you can easily search for available plugins there:

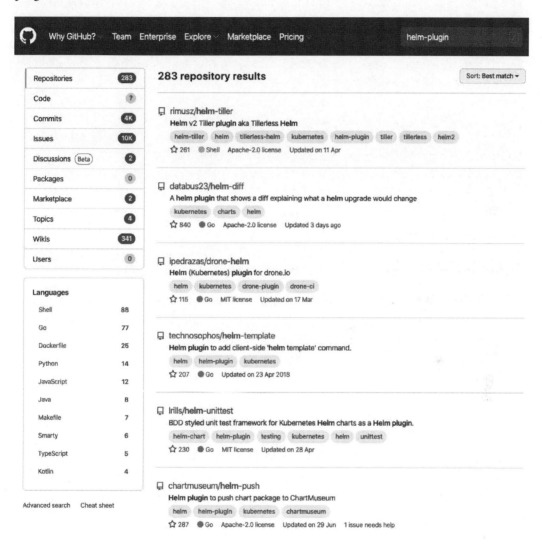

Figure 9.20 – Helm plugins search on GitHub

In the preceding screenshot `https://github.com/search?q=helm-plugin` was used to search for Helm plugins in GitHub.

Let's see how easy it is to install a Helm plugin:

```
$ helm plugin list
```

The output of the preceding command is shown in the following screenshot:

```
 code $ helm plugin list
NAME    VERSION DESCRIPTION
 code $ helm plugin install https://github.com/databus23/helm-diff
Downloading https://github.com/databus23/helm-diff/releases/download/v3.1.3/helm-diff-mac
os.tgz
  % Total    % Received % Xferd  Average Speed   Time    Time     Time  Current
                                 Dload  Upload   Total   Spent    Left  Speed
100   643  100   643    0     0   1400      0 --:--:-- --:--:-- --:--:--  1397
100 14.7M  100 14.7M    0     0  4373k      0  0:00:03  0:00:03 --:--:-- 6901k
Preparing to install into /Users/rimasm/tmp/helm_home/data/helm/plugins/helm-diff
helm-diff installed into /Users/rimasm/tmp/helm_home/data/helm/plugins/helm-diff/helm-dif
f

The Helm Diff Plugin

* Shows a diff explaining what a helm upgrade would change:
    This fetches the currently deployed version of a release
  and compares it to a local chart plus values. This can be
  used visualize what changes a helm upgrade will perform.

* Shows a diff explaining what had changed between two revisions:
    This fetches previously deployed versions of a release
  and compares them. This can be used visualize what changes
  were made during revision change.

* Shows a diff explaining what a helm rollback would change:
    This fetches the currently deployed version of a release
  and compares it to adeployed versions of a release, that you
  want to rollback. This can be used visualize what changes a
  helm rollback will perform.

Usage:
  diff [flags]
  diff [command]
```

Figure 9.21 – Helm plugin helm-diff being installed

In the preceding command, helm plugin list, we checked for installed plugins, then we used helm plugin install https://github.com/databus23/helm-diff to install the helm-diff plugin. The preceding plugin installation output was cut as the installed plugin prints a lot of information.

Let's check the plugins list:

```
$ helm plugin list
```

The output of the preceding command is shown in the following screenshot:

```
 code $ helm plugin list
NAME    VERSION DESCRIPTION
diff    3.1.3   Preview helm upgrade changes as a diff
```

Figure 9.22 – Helm plugin list

We see that the `diff` plugin is installed, which is basically a new Helm command: `helm diff`.

We are not going to check how `helm diff` works, but it is a very handy one as you can check the differences between the installed and new chart versions.

Let's install one more:

```
$ helm plugin install https://github.com/instrumenta/helm-kubeval
```

The output of the preceding command is shown in the following screenshot:

```
 code $ helm plugin install https://github.com/instrumenta/helm-kubeval
Installing helm-kubeval v0.13.0 ...
x LICENSE
x README.md
x kubeval
helm-kubeval 0.13.0 is installed.

See https://kubeval.instrumenta.dev for help getting started.
Installed plugin: kubeval
 code $ helm plugin list
NAME    VERSION DESCRIPTION
diff    3.1.3   Preview helm upgrade changes as a diff
kubeval 0.13.0  "Validate Helm charts against the Kubernetes schemas"
 code $ helm kubeval --help
Validate a Kubernetes YAML file against the relevant schema

Usage:
  kubeval <file> [file...] [flags]
```

Figure 9.23 – helm plugin install helm-kubeval

The preceding command, `helm plugin install https://github.com/instrumenta/helm-kubeval`, installed the `kubeval` plugin, which validates Helm charts against Kubernetes schemas.

Let's validate the `nginx` chart that we created with `helm create` before:

```
$ helm kubeval nginx
```

The output of the preceding command is shown in the following screenshot:

```
 code $ helm kubeval nginx
The file nginx/templates/serviceaccount.yaml contains a valid ServiceAccount
The file nginx/templates/service.yaml contains a valid Service
The file nginx/templates/deployment.yaml contains a valid Deployment
The file nginx/templates/tests/test-connection.yaml contains a valid Pod
```

Figure 9.24 – Validating the nginx chart with the kubeval plugin

The preceding `helm kubeval nginx` command validated the `nginx` chart – as we can see, it's all green, so no issues there. This plugin is a good addition to the `helm lint` command, and the combination of both gives you nice tooling to check charts with.

Now, we know how to extend Helm with extra features, as one tool cannot have everything. Plugins are easy to write as well, and you can learn that in your own time, of course.

Summary

In this chapter, we have learned how to use Helm for installing, upgrading, rolling back releases, checking chart templates' output, creating a chart, linting a chart, and extending Helm with plugins.

Helm is a powerful tool with which you can deploy both simple and complex Kubernetes applications. It will help you to deploy real-world applications, especially as there are so many different charts ready to use from many Helm repositories.

In the last chapter of this book, we're going to learn `kubectl` best practices and `kubectl` commands for Docker users.

10

kubectl Best Practices and Docker Commands

In the previous chapter, we learned about Helm, which is a Kubernetes package manager. In this last chapter of our book, we are going to learn about a few `kubectl` best practices.

In this chapter, we will learn how to use shell aliases to shorten `kubectl` commands, and other handy tips for using `kubectl` commands, as well.

We will also check some equivalent commands in Docker for some `kubectl` commands, especially the ones that are handy to know for new Kubernetes users who are familiar with Docker commands and want to know about similar commands in `kubectl`.

In this chapter, we're going to cover the following main topics:

- Using shell aliases for kubectl commands
- Similar Docker commands in kubectl

Using shell aliases for kubectl commands

Typing kubectl with a command every time is both boring and time-consuming. You can use kubectl command completion in the Bash and Zsh shells, which helps of course, but it is still not as quick as using aliases.

Let's overview a list of some handy kubectl commands and use them with aliases that you can put in the zsh_aliases or bash_aliases files, depending on which shell you are using:

- k for kubectl—this speaks for itself.

- kg for kubectl get—this is useful to get a list of pods, deployments, statefulsets, services, nodes, and other details, as shown in the following example command:

```
$ kg nodes
```

The output of the preceding command is shown in the following screenshot:

Figure 10.1 – kg nodes output

The preceding screenshot shows a list of available Kubernetes nodes in the cluster by running the $ kg nodes command.

- kd for kubectl describe—this is useful to describe pods, deployments, statefulsets, services, nodes, and so on.

- kga for kubectl get all—this shows a list of pods, deployments, statefulsets, services, and resources in the currently set namespace. You can also provide the -n flag to specify the namespace or -A to show resources in all namespaces:

```
$ kga
```

The output of the preceding command is shown in the following screenshot:

Figure 10.2 – kga output

The preceding screenshot shows the output of the `kga` alias with the resources found in the current namespace.

- `krga` for `kubectl really get all`—this shows the list of all resources including secrets, events, and more in the currently set namespace. You can also provide the `-n` flag to specify the namespace or `-A` to show all resources from all namespaces.

- `kp` for `kubectl get pods -o wide`—this shows the list of pods in the current namespace. The `-o wide` flag shows a given pod's assigned IP and the node it has been scheduled to:

```
$ k get pods
$ kp
```

The output of the preceding command is shown in the following screenshot:

```
▶ code $ k get pods
NAME                      READY   STATUS    RESTARTS   AGE
nginx-fcb5d6b64-x4kwg     1/1     Running   0          6d22h
▶ code $ kp
NAME                      READY   STATUS    RESTARTS   AGE    IP          NODE
nginx-fcb5d6b64-x4kwg     1/1     Running   0          6d22h  10.8.0.2    gke-kubectl-lab-we-app-pool-1302ab74-cwjf
```

Figure 10.3 – kgak get pods output

The preceding screenshot shows the output of the `k get pods` and `kp` aliases.

- `kap` for `kubectl get pods -A -o wide`—this is a similar alias to `kp`, but shows the pods in all namespaces.

- `ka` for `kubectl apply -f`—you can use this to create/update a deployment:

```
$ ka nginx.yaml
```

- `kei` for `kubectl exec -it`—this executes into the running pod's shell:

```
$ kei nginx-fcb5d6b64-x4kwg - bash
```

The output of the preceding command is shown in the following screenshot:

```
▶ code $ kp
NAME                      READY   STATUS    RESTARTS   AGE    IP
nginx-fcb5d6b64-x4kwg     1/1     Running   0          6d22h  10.8.0.2
▶ code $ kei nginx-fcb5d6b64-x4kwg bash -- bash
root@nginx-fcb5d6b64-x4kwg:/# []
```

Figure 10.4 – kei output

The preceding screenshot shows the output of `kei nginx-fcb5d6b64-x4kwg bash - bash`.

- `ke` for `kubectl exec`—this executes a command in the running pod:

```
$ ke nginx-fcb5d6b64-x4kwg -- ls -alh
```

The output of the preceding command is shown in the following screenshot:

```
▶ code $ kp
NAME                       READY  STATUS   RESTARTS  AGE    IP
nginx-fcb5d6b64-x4kwg      1/1    Running  0         6d22h  10.8.0.2
▶ code $ ke nginx-fcb5d6b64-x4kwg -- ls -alh
total 76K
drwxr-xr-x   1 root root 4.0K Sep 13 13:16 .
drwxr-xr-x   1 root root 4.0K Sep 13 13:16 ..
-rwxr-xr-x   1 root root    0 Sep 13 13:16 .dockerenv
drwxr-xr-x   2 root root 4.0K Aug 12  2019 bin
drwxr-xr-x   2 root root 4.0K Mar 28  2019 boot
drwxr-xr-x   5 root root  360 Sep 13 13:16 dev
drwxr-xr-x   1 root root 4.0K Sep 13 13:16 etc
drwxr-xr-x   2 root root 4.0K Mar 28  2019 home
drwxr-xr-x   1 root root 4.0K Aug 12  2019 lib
drwxr-xr-x   2 root root 4.0K Aug 12  2019 lib64
drwxr-xr-x   2 root root 4.0K Aug 12  2019 media
drwxr-xr-x   2 root root 4.0K Aug 12  2019 mnt
drwxr-xr-x   2 root root 4.0K Aug 12  2019 opt
dr-xr-xr-x 146 root root    0 Sep 13 13:16 proc
drwx------   1 root root 4.0K Sep 13 14:47 root
drwxr-xr-x   1 root root 4.0K Sep 13 13:16 run
drwxr-xr-x   2 root root 4.0K Aug 12  2019 sbin
drwxr-xr-x   2 root root 4.0K Aug 12  2019 srv
dr-xr-xr-x  12 root root    0 Sep 13 14:49 sys
drwxrwxrwt   1 root root 4.0K Aug 14  2019 tmp
drwxr-xr-x   1 root root 4.0K Aug 12  2019 usr
drwxr-xr-x   1 root root 4.0K Aug 12  2019 var
```

Figure 10.5 – ke output

The preceding screenshot shows the output of `ke nginx-fcb5d6b64-x4kwg bash – ls -alh`.

- `ktn` for `watch kubectl top nodes`—use this to watch a node's resource consumption:

```
$ ktn
```

The output of the preceding command is shown in the following screenshot:

```
Every 2.0s: kubectl top nodes

NAME                                        CPU(cores)  CPU%  MEMORY(bytes)  MEMORY%
gke-kubectl-lab-we-app-pool-1302ab74-cwjf   99m         10%   572Mi          21%
```

Figure 10.6 – ktn output

The preceding screenshot shows the output of `ktn` with the list of nodes and their respective resource usages.

- `ktp` for `watch kubectl top pods`—use this to watch a pod's resources consumption:

```
$ ktp
```

The output of the preceding command is shown in the following screenshot:

```
Every 2.0s: kubectl top pods

NAME                        CPU(cores)   MEMORY(bytes)
nginx-fcb5d6b64-x4kwg       1m           2Mi
```

Figure 10.7 – ktp output

The preceding screenshot shows the output of `ktp` with the list of pods and their resource usages.

- `kpf` for `kubectl port-forward`—use this to do a port forward for the pod so we can access the pod from `localhost`:

```
$ kpf nginx-fcb5d6b64-x4kwg 8080
```

The output of the preceding command is shown in the following screenshot:

```
▸ code $ kp
NAME                   READY   STATUS    RESTARTS   AGE     IP          NODE
nginx-fcb5d6b64-x4kwg  1/1     Running   0          6d22h   10.8.0.2    gke-kubectl-lab-we-app-pool-1302ab74-cwjf
▸ code $ kpf nginx-fcb5d6b64-x4kwg 8080
Forwarding from 127.0.0.1:8080 -> 8080
Forwarding from [::1]:8080 -> 8080
```

Figure 10.8 – kpf output

The preceding screenshot shows the output of `kpf` with port forwarding set to port `8080`.

- `kl` for `kubectl logs`—this shows the logs of a pod or deployment:

```
$ kl deploy/nginx --tail 10
```

The output of the preceding command is shown in the following screenshot:

```
▸ code $ k get deploy
NAME    READY   UP-TO-DATE   AVAILABLE   AGE
nginx   1/1     1            1           8d
▸ code $ kl deploy/nginx --tail 10
10.8.0.1 - - [13/Sep/2020:15:02:21 +0000] "GET / HTTP/1.1" 200 612 "-" "kube-probe/1.17+" "-"
10.8.0.1 - - [13/Sep/2020:15:02:23 +0000] "GET / HTTP/1.1" 200 612 "-" "kube-probe/1.17+" "-"
10.8.0.1 - - [13/Sep/2020:15:02:31 +0000] "GET / HTTP/1.1" 200 612 "-" "kube-probe/1.17+" "-"
10.8.0.1 - - [13/Sep/2020:15:02:33 +0000] "GET / HTTP/1.1" 200 612 "-" "kube-probe/1.17+" "-"
10.8.0.1 - - [13/Sep/2020:15:02:41 +0000] "GET / HTTP/1.1" 200 612 "-" "kube-probe/1.17+" "-"
10.8.0.1 - - [13/Sep/2020:15:02:43 +0000] "GET / HTTP/1.1" 200 612 "-" "kube-probe/1.17+" "-"
10.8.0.1 - - [13/Sep/2020:15:02:51 +0000] "GET / HTTP/1.1" 200 612 "-" "kube-probe/1.17+" "-"
10.8.0.1 - - [13/Sep/2020:15:02:53 +0000] "GET / HTTP/1.1" 200 612 "-" "kube-probe/1.17+" "-"
10.8.0.1 - - [13/Sep/2020:15:03:01 +0000] "GET / HTTP/1.1" 200 612 "-" "kube-probe/1.17+" "-"
10.8.0.1 - - [13/Sep/2020:15:03:03 +0000] "GET / HTTP/1.1" 200 612 "-" "kube-probe/1.17+" "-"
```

Figure 10.9 – kl output

The preceding screenshot shows the output of k1 with the logs for the nginx deployment.

Also, you can add the following to your list:

- d: docker

- kz: kustomize

- h: helm

An example snippet of .zsh_aliases is shown in the following code block:

```
$ cat .zsh_aliases
# aliases
alias a="atom ."
alias c="code ."
alias d="docker"
alias h="helm"
alias k="kubectl"
alias ke="kubectl exec -it"
alias kc="kubectl create -f"
alias ka="kubectl apply -f"
alias kd="kubectl describe"
alias kl="kubectl logs"
alias kg="kubectl get"
alias kp="kubectl get pods -o wide"
alias kap="kubectl get pods --all-namespaces -o wide"
alias ktn="watch kubectl top nodes"
alias ktp="watch kubectl top pods"
alias ktc="watch kubectl top pods --containers"
alias kpf="kubectl port-forward"
alias kcx="kubectx"
alias kns="kubectl-ns"
```

Using aliases will help you to be more productive by typing a few letters instead of a few words. Also, not all commands are easy to remember, so using aliases will help to overcome that too.

Similar Docker commands in kubectl

The following is a list of the most useful Docker commands, followed by their equivalents in `kubectl`.

Getting information is done with the following commands:

- `docker info`
- `kubectl cluster-info`

Getting version information is done with the following commands:

- `docker version`
- `kubectl version`

Running a container and exposing its port is done with the following commands:

- `docker run -d --restart=always --name nginx -p 80:80 nginx`
- `kubectl create deployment --image=nginx nginx`
- `kubectl expose deployment nginx --port=80 --name=nginx`

Getting container logs is done with the following commands:

- `docker logs --f <container name>`
- `kubectl logs --f <pod name>`

Executing into a running container/pod shell is done with the following commands:

- `docker exec -it <container name> /bin/bash`
- `kubectl exec -it <pod name>`

Getting a list of containers/pods is done with the following commands:

- `docker ps -a`
- `kubectl get pods`

Stopping and removing a container/pod is done with the following commands:

- `docker stop <container name> && docker rm <container name>`
- `kubectl delete deployment <deployment name>`
- `kubectl delete pod <pod name>`

We have now learned the most useful `kubectl` commands for Docker users, which should speed up your learning curve with `kubectl` and will become useful commands in your daily work.

Summary

In this final chapter, we learned some `kubectl` best practices by examining how to use aliases to run various commands with `kubectl`, and then saw some equivalents for Docker commands in `kubectl`.

Using aliases shortens the time required for typing, and of course, aliases are easier to remember instead of some long commands.

Throughout this book, we have learned a lot of useful information, such as how to install `kubectl`; getting information about the cluster and nodes; installing, updating, and debugging an application; working with `kubectl` plugins; and also learned about Kustomize and Helm.

I hope the book will help you to master Kubernetes, `kubectl`, and Helm.

Other Books You May Enjoy

If you enjoyed this book, you may be interested in these other books by Packt:

Learn Kubernetes Security

Kaizhe Huang and Pranjal Jumde

ISBN: 978-1-83921-650-3

- Understand the basics of Kubernetes architecture and networking

- Gain insights into different security integrations provided by the Kubernetes platform

- Delve into Kubernetes' threat modeling and security domains

- Explore different security configurations from a variety of practical examples

- Get to grips with using and deploying open source tools to protect your deployments

- Discover techniques to mitigate or prevent known Kubernetes hacks

Learn Helm

Andrew Block and Austin Dewey

ISBN: 978-1-83921-429-5

- Develop an enterprise automation strategy on Kubernetes using Helm
- Create easily consumable and configurable Helm charts
- Use Helm in orchestration tooling and Kubernetes operators
- Explore best practices for application delivery and life cycle management
- Leverage Helm in a secure and stable manner that is fit for your enterprise
- Discover the ins and outs of automation with Helm

Leave a review - let other readers know what you think

Please share your thoughts on this book with others by leaving a review on the site that you bought it from. If you purchased the book from Amazon, please leave us an honest review on this book's Amazon page. This is vital so that other potential readers can see and use your unbiased opinion to make purchasing decisions, we can understand what our customers think about our products, and our authors can see your feedback on the title that they have worked with Packt to create. It will only take a few minutes of your time, but is valuable to other potential customers, our authors, and Packt. Thank you!

Index

Printed in Great Britain
by Amazon

78649045R10079